In June 2011, Julian Assange re

of Google, Eric Schmidt, arrived from America at Ellingham Hall, the country residence in Norfolk, England where Assange was living under house arrest.

For several hours the besieged leader of the world's most famous insurgent publishing organization and the billionaire head of the world's largest information empire locked horns. The two men debated the political problems faced by society, and the technological solutions engendered by the global network—from the Arab Spring to Bitcoin. They outlined radically opposing perspectives: for Assange, the liberating power of the Internet is based on its freedom and statelessness. For Schmidt, emancipation is at one with US foreign policy objectives and is driven by connecting non-Western countries to Western companies and markets. These differences embodied a tug-of-war over the Internet's future that has only gathered force subsequently.

When Google Met WikiLeaks presents the story of Assange and Schmidt's encounter. Both fascinating and alarming, it contains an edited transcript of their conversation and extensive, new material, written by Assange specifically for this book, providing the best available summary of his vision for the future of the Internet.

When Google Met WikiLeaks

JULIAN ASSANGE

O/R

OR Books

New York · London

Published by OR Books, New York and London
Visit our website at www.orbooks.com

First printing 2014

First published for the book trade in 2016 by OR Books/Counterpoint

Cataloging-in-Publication data is available from the Library of Congress.
A catalog record for this book is available from the British Library.

ISBN 978-1-944869-11-3 paperback
ISBN 978-1-944869-24-3 e-book

This book is set in the typeface Minion. Typeset by Lapiz Digital, Chennai, India.

CONTENTS

For my family, whom I love and miss very much

"Headbone connected to the headphones
Headphones connected to the iPhone
iPhone connected to the Internet
Connected to the Google
Connected to the government"

—MIA, "The Message"

BEYOND GOOD AND "DON'T BE EVIL"

Eric Schmidt is an influential figure, even among the parade of powerful characters with whom I have had to cross paths since I founded WikiLeaks. In mid-May 2011 I was under house arrest in rural Norfolk, about three hours' drive northeast of London. The crackdown against our work was in full swing and every wasted moment seemed like an eternity. It was hard to get my attention. But when my colleague Joseph Farrell told me the executive chairman of Google wanted to make an appointment with me, I was listening.

In some ways the higher echelons of Google seemed more distant and obscure to me than the halls of Washington. We had been locking horns with senior US officials for years by that point. The mystique had worn off. But the power centers growing up in Silicon Valley were still opaque and I was suddenly conscious of an opportunity to understand and influence what was becoming the most influential company on earth. Schmidt had taken over as CEO of Google in 2001 and built it into an empire.[1]

---

1. The company is now valued at $400 billion and employs 49,829 people. The valuation at the end of 2011 was $200 billion with 33,077 employees. See "Investor Relations: 2012 Financial Tables," Google, archive.today/Iux4M For the first quarter of 2014, see "Investor Relations: 2014 Financial Tables," Google, archive.today/35IeZ

I was intrigued that the mountain would come to Muhammad. But it was not until well after Schmidt and his companions had been and gone that I came to understand who had really visited me.

* * *

The stated reason for the visit was a book. Schmidt was penning a treatise with Jared Cohen, the director of Google Ideas, an outfit that describes itself as Google's in-house "think/do tank." I knew little else about Cohen at the time. In fact, Cohen had moved to Google from the US State Department in 2010. He had been a fast-talking "Generation Y" ideas man at State under two US administrations, a courtier from the world of policy think tanks and institutes, poached in his early twenties. He became a senior advisor for Secretaries of State Rice and Clinton. At State, on the Policy Planning Staff, Cohen was soon christened "Condi's party-starter," channeling buzzwords from Silicon Valley into US policy circles and producing delightful rhetorical concoctions such as "Public Diplomacy 2.0."[2] On his Council on Foreign Relations adjunct staff page he listed his expertise as "terrorism; radicalization; impact of connection technologies on 21st century statecraft; Iran."[3]

---

2.   For a strong essay on Schmidt and Cohen's book that discusses similar themes, and that provoked some of the research for this book, see Joseph L. Flatley, "Being cynical: Julian Assange, Eric Schmidt, and the year's weirdest book," *Verge*, 7 June 2013, archive.today/gfLEr

3.   Jared Cohen's profile on the Council on Foreign Relations website, archive.today/pkgQN

It was Cohen who, while he was still at the Department of State, was said to have emailed Twitter CEO Jack Dorsey to delay scheduled maintenance in order to assist the aborted 2009 uprising in Iran.[4] His documented love affair with Google began the same year, when he befriended Eric Schmidt as they together surveyed the post-occupation wreckage of Baghdad. Just months later, Schmidt re-created Cohen's natural habitat within Google itself by engineering a "think/do tank" based in New York and appointing Cohen as its head. Google Ideas was born.

Later that year the two co-wrote a policy piece for the Council on Foreign Relations' journal *Foreign Affairs*, praising the reformative potential of Silicon Valley technologies as an instrument of US foreign policy.[5] Describing what they called "coalitions of the connected,"[6] Schmidt and Cohen claimed that

> Democratic states that have built coalitions of their militaries have the capacity to do the same with their connection technologies. . . .

4. Shawn Donnan, "Think again," *Financial Times*, 8 July 2011, archive. today/ndbmj See also Rick Schmitt, "Diplomacy 2.0," *Stanford Alumni*, May/June 2011, archive.today/Kidpc

5. Eric Schmidt and Jared Cohen, "The Digital Disruption: Connectivity and the Diffusion of Power," *Foreign Affairs*, November/December 2010, archive.today/R13l2

6. "Coalitions of the connected" is a phrase apparently designed to resonate with the "coalition of the willing," which was used to designate the 2003 US-led alliance of states preparing to invade Iraq without UN Security Council approval.

They offer a new way to exercise the *duty to protect* citizens around the world [emphasis added].[7]

In the same piece they argued that "this technology is overwhelmingly provided by the private sector."

In February 2011, less than two months after that article was published, Egyptian president Hosni Mubarak was ousted by a popular revolution. Egypt had been a US client, its military dictatorship propped up by Washington to support America's "geopolitical

---

7.   The phrase "duty to protect" is redolent of "responsibility to protect," or, in its abbreviated form, "R2P." R2P is a highly controversial "emerging norm" in international law. R2P leverages human rights discourse to mandate "humanitarian intervention" by "the international community" in countries where the civilian population is deemed to be at risk. For US liberals who eschew the naked imperialism of Paul Wolfowitz (on which see Patrick E. Tyler, "U.S. strategy plan calls for insuring no rivals develop," *New York Times*, 8 March 1992, archive.today/Rin1g), R2P is the justification of choice for Western military action in the Middle East and elsewhere, as evidenced by its ubiquity in the push to invade Libya in 2011 and Syria in 2013. Jared Cohen's former superior at the US State Department, Anne-Marie Slaughter, has called it "the most important shift in our conception of sovereignty since the Treaty of Westphalia in 1648." See her praise for the book *Responsibility to Protect: The Global Moral Compact for the 21st Century*, edited by Richard H. Cooper and Juliette Voïnov Kohler, on the website of the publisher Palgrave Macmillan, archive.today/0dmMq

For a critical essay on R2P see Noam Chomsky's statement on the doctrine to the UN General Assembly. Noam Chomsky, "Statement by Professor Noam Chomsky to the United Nations General Assembly Thematic Dialogue on Responsibility to Protect," United Nations, New York, 23 July 2009, is.gd/bLx3uU

See also "Responsibility to protect: An idea whose time has come—and gone?" *Economist*, 23 July 2009, archive.today/K2WZJ

interests in the region."[8] During the initial stages of the revolution, Western political elites had backed Mubarak. US vice president Biden, who only a month earlier had claimed that "Julian Assange" was a "high-tech terrorist," now informed the world that Hosni Mubarak was "not a dictator" and stressed that he should not resign.[9] Former UK prime minister Tony Blair insisted that Mubarak was "immensely courageous and a force for good."[10] For Secretary of State Hillary Clinton, the Mubaraks were "family friends."[11]

Under the surface, as a close reading of its internal cable traffic shows, the State Department had for years bet on both horses, supporting and co-opting elements of Egyptian civil society even as it helped to keep Mubarak in power. But when the US establishment realized that Hosni was on the way out, it scrambled for alternatives. It first tried to elevate its secretly preferred successor, Omar Suleiman—the much-hated domestic intelligence chief. But the State Department's own diplomatic correspondence from Cairo, which we were publishing in volume at the time, provided a frank appraisal of his background. Suleiman was Egypt's torturer in chief, the CIA's main man in Egypt, and Israel's approved choice

---

8. Bridget Johnson, "Biden: Mubarak not a dictator, protests not like Eastern Europe," *The Hill*, 28 January 2011, archive.today/L7EcI

9. Ibid.

10. Chris McGreal, "Tony Blair: Mubarak is 'immensely courageous and a force for good,'" *Guardian*, 2 February 2011, archive.today/SIsmb

11. "Secretary Clinton in 2009: 'I really consider President and Mrs. Mubarak to be friends of my family,'" ABC News, 31 January 2011, archive.today/8NAoz

for Mubarak's replacement.[12] For these and other reasons Suleiman lost international support and Egyptians rejected him just as they had rejected Mubarak. Never keen to back a loser, the United States pivoted, trying to plant itself in front of the crowd. Its former hesitancy was readily forgotten, and the long, hard road to the Egyptian revolution was spun by Hillary Clinton as a triumph for American technology corporations, and later, for the State Department itself.[13]

Suddenly everyone wanted to be at the intersection point between US global power and social media, and Schmidt and Cohen had already staked out the territory. With the working title "The Empire of the Mind," they began expanding their article to book length, and sought audiences with the big names of global tech and global power as part of their research.

They said they wanted to interview me. I agreed.

A date was set for June.

* * *

---

12. Richard Smallteacher, "Egypt–Egypt–U.S. intelligence collaboration with Omar Suleiman 'most successful,'" WikiLeaks, 1 February 2011, archive.today/neBhy

13. See "Secretary of State Hillary Clinton's Speech on Internet Freedom *updated*," *Secretary Clinton Blog*, 15 February 2011, archive.today/nChdl
    Egyptian activists themselves were usually off-message: "While we appreciated the training we received through the NGOs sponsored by the U.S. government, and it did help us in our struggles, we are also aware that the same government also trained the state security investigative service, which was responsible for the harassment and jailing of many of us," Egyptian activist Basem Fathy told the *New York Times* in April 2011. Ron Nixon, "U.S. Groups Helped Nurture Arab Uprisings," *New York Times*, 14 April 2011, archive.today/bJyGP

By the time June came around there was already a lot to talk about. That summer WikiLeaks was still grinding through the release of US diplomatic cables, publishing thousands of them every week. When, seven months earlier, we had first started releasing the cables, Hillary Clinton had denounced the publication as "an attack on the international community" that would "tear at the fabric" of government. She was, in a way, right.

In many countries, the "fabric" Clinton referred to had been woven from lies: the more authoritarian the country, the bigger the lies. The more a power faction relied on the US to prop up its power, the more it whispered into American ears about its factional rivals. This pattern was repeated in capital cities all over the world: a capricious global system of secret loyalties, owed favors, and false consensus, of saying one thing in public and the opposite in private. The scale and geographic diversity of our publications overwhelmed the State Department's ability to handle the crisis. Threads between players snapped, leaving gaps through which decades of resentment would pour.[14]

The "tears in the fabric" of government appeared almost immediately in North Africa. On November 28, 2010, the first cables were released into an already volatile political environment. The corruption of the regime of Zine el-Abidine Ben Ali was no secret in Tunisia, where the population suffered widespread poverty, unemployment, and government repression, while regime favorites hosted lavish parties and looked after their friends. But the State Department's

---

14. "Clinton on a WikiLeaks 'apology tour,'" UPI, 10 January 2011, archive.today/AYRCx

own internal documentation of the decadence of the Ben Ali government began to instigate public anger and calls to action among Tunisians. Ben Ali's propaganda minister, Oussama Romdhani, later confessed that our leaks were "the coup de grâce, the thing that broke the Ben Ali system."[15] The regime began to censor the cables online, further enraging the public. WikiLeaks, *Al Akhbar*, and *Le Monde* disappeared from the Tunisian internet, replaced with "Ammar 404": "Page not found." The Tunisian publisher Nawaat.org fought back, disseminating translations of the cables under the radar of the Tunisian censorship system. For twenty days the mood simmered until, on December 17, the

---

15. Tunisian publisher Naawat's Sami Ben Gharbia put it this way: "Twenty days passed between the release of the Tunileaks cables, on November 28th, 2010, and the start of the Arab Spring, on December 17th, 2010. That was the day a poor street vendor named Mohamed Bouazizi set himself on fire. In a chat with a British journalist this year, Ben Ali's propaganda minister Oussama Romdhani confessed that *'Tunileaks was the coup de grâce, the thing that broke the Ben Ali system.'* It wasn't the information about corruption and cronyism, Tunisians didn't need Tunileaks to tell them their country was corrupt. Tunisians had been gossiping and joking about the corruption for years. What was different was the psychological effect of an establishment confronted so publicly with its ugly own image. It was that the government knew that all people knew, inside and outside the country, how corrupt and authoritarian it was. And the one telling the story wasn't a dissident or a political conspirator. It was the U.S. State department, a supposed ally." Sami Ben Gharbia, "Chelsea Manning and the Arab Spring," *Nawaat*, 28 February 2014, archive.today/pw0p9

    Another article by Sami Ben Gharbia, published just months before the Arab Spring, is strong on the broader topic of the US "internet freedom" agenda in the Middle East and North Africa. Sami Ben Gharbia, "The Internet Freedom Fallacy and the Arab Digital Activism," *Nawaat*, 17 September 2010, archive.today/aoTrj

young fruit seller Mohamed Bouazizi, driven to despair by corrupt municipal officials, set himself on fire. In death he was transformed into a symbol, and open rebellion spilled onto the streets.

The protests raged over the New Year. On January 10, Tunisia was still in revolt when Hillary Clinton embarked on what she described as her global WikiLeaks "apology tour," starting in the Middle East.[16] Four days later the Tunisian government fell. Eleven days after that, the civil unrest spread to Egypt. The images were beamed throughout the region on unblockable satellite television by Qatar's Al Jazeera network. Within a month there were "days of rage" and civil uprisings in Yemen, Libya, Syria, and Bahrain, and large-scale protests in Algeria, Iraq, Jordan, Kuwait, Morocco, and Sudan. Even Saudi Arabia and Oman saw demonstrations. The year 2011 became one of serious political awakenings, crackdowns, and opportunistic military interventions. In January Muammar Gaddafi denounced WikiLeaks.[17] By the end of the year he would be dead.

The wave of revolutionary excitement soon washed over Europe and elsewhere. By the time of my meeting with Schmidt in June, the Puerta del Sol was occupied and protesters were facing down black-clad riot police in squares all across Spain. There were encampments

---

16. "Clinton on a WikiLeaks 'apology tour,'" UPI, 10 January 2011, archive.today/AYRCx

17. Brian Whitaker, "Gaddafi versus Kleenex," 18 January 2011, available on al-bab.com under "Libya: The fall of Colonel Gaddafi," archive.today/lxF1u

    Jillian C. York, "Qaddafi's View of the Internet in Tunisia," jilliancyork.com, 16 January 2011, archive.today/GFRQC

in Israel. Peru had seen protests and a change of government.[18] The Chilean students' movement had taken to the streets. The state capitol in Madison, Wisconsin, had been besieged by tens of thousands of people standing for workers' rights.[19] Riots were about to erupt in Greece, and then in London.

Alongside the changes on the streets, the internet was rapidly transitioning from an apathetic communications medium into a *demos—a people* with a shared culture, shared values, and shared aspirations. It had become a place where history happens, a place people identified with and even felt they *came from*.

The US government's treatment of the alleged source of the State Department cables, Chelsea Manning, had been witnessed by the whole world. By June a global campaign, coordinated over

---

18.   Greg Grandin, "With Ollanta Humala's Win, Peru Joins Latin America's Left Turn," *Nation*, 7 June 2011, archive.today/8cvxx
         See also Nikolas Kozloff, "WikiLeaks cables: The great equaliser in Peru," *Al Jazeera*, 2 June 2011, archive.today/wBacn

19.   The guitarist and songwriter Tom Morello (Rage Against the Machine, Audioslave, the Nightwatchman, Street Sweeper Social Club, "Multi-Viral" by Calle 13 featuring Tom Morello, Julian Assange, and Kamilya Jubran), while playing to the crowd at the Wisconsin protests, read out a letter of solidarity sent to him by one of the organizers from Tahrir Square, Moar Eletrebi, which read, "To our friends in Madison, Wisconsin: We wish you could see first hand the change we have made here. Justice is beautiful, but justice is never free. The beauty of Tahrir Square you can have anywhere, on any street corner, in your city, or in your heart. So hold on tightly, and don't let go, and breathe deep Wisconsin! Our good fortune is on the breeze, in the Mid West, and in the Middle East. Breathe deep, Wisconsin, because justice is in the air, and may the spirit of Tahrir Square be in every beating heart on the streets of Madison today." Tom Morello, "Frostbite and Freedom: Tom Morello on the Battle of Madison," *Rolling Stone*, 25 February 2011, archive.today/nTB6h

the internet, had managed to pressure the US government to stop torturing her.[20]

The US financial blockade against WikiLeaks had provoked massive denial-of-service protests from a once apolitical internet youth. Anonymous—once an obscure internet meme—had become a battering ram for the internet's emergent political ideology.

In a spectacular electronic intrusion and information dump, sympathetic hackers operating under the Anonymous banner had exposed a $2-million-a-month subversion campaign targeting WikiLeaks and its supporters (including reporter Glenn Greenwald), which had been prepared by a group of private security contractors on behalf of the Bank of America.[21]

---

20. Manning spent much of the first year of her detention without trial in solitary confinement at a US Marines brig in Quantico, Virginia, under conditions described by UN Special Rapporteur on Torture Juan Mendez as "cruel, inhumane and degrading" and possibly amounting to torture.

Manning's defense team suggested the treatment had been carried out to coerce a "confession" implicating WikiLeaks. President Barack Obama said that Manning's conditions were "appropriate and meeting our basic standards." Three hundred law professors, including Harvard's Laurence Tribe, whose former students include Obama, denounced the abuse. The State Department's spokesman Philip J. Crowley said that the Pentagon's treatment of Manning was "ridiculous, counterproductive and stupid," and then resigned.

An international campaign succeeded in putting diplomatic pressure on the US government, after which Manning was moved to Fort Leavenworth, Kansas, and the US Marines brig at Quantico, Virginia, was shut down permanently.

For more details on the inhumane treatment of Chelsea Manning, see "Background on US v. WikiLeaks," page 205.

21. This is known as the HBGary Federal scandal. For details, see "Background on US v. WikiLeaks," page 205.

Barrett Brown, a talented young freelance journalist, had begun the investigative work into this state-security axis that would eventually land him in a US prison.[22] Bitcoin had gone from being worthless

---

22. Barrett Brown is a freelance journalist whose investigation into the security industry brought the US authorities down on his head. Brown was arrested in September 2012 and denied bail. In October 2012 he was indicted while he remained in prison; the three charges related to threats he was alleged to have made against an FBI agent. In December 2012 he was indicted on twelve additional charges relating to his work as a journalist covering the alleged hack a year previously of the Texas intelligence firm Stratfor. See Glenn Greenwald, "The persecution of Barrett Brown—and how to fight it," *Guardian*, 21 March 2013, archive.today/tUnJ9

See also Douglas Lucas, "Barrett Brown's new book 'Keep Rootin' for Putin' skewers mainstream media pundits," *Vice*, 25 February 2014, archive.today/oS5qv

See also Christian Stork, "The Saga Of Barrett Brown: Inside Anonymous and the War on Secrecy," *WhoWhatWhy*, 21 February 2013, archive.today/mUtJE

The maximum possible sentence deriving from the charges against Brown was 105 years. See Kristin Bergman, "Adding up to 105: The Charges Against Barrett Brown," Digital Media Law Project, 6 August 2013, archive.today/TQrdR

One of the charges alleging a threat against an FBI agent related to a tweet Brown had posted containing the words "Dead men can't leak stuff… illegally shoot the son of a bitch." In fact, this was not a threat to an FBI agent—Brown was quoting an explicit call for my assassination, originally uttered by the Fox News commentator Bob Beckel on television on 6 December 2010. Although Brown has been charged for quoting Beckel's words in order to criticize them, Beckel remains unindicted. See "Fox News' Bob Beckel Calls For 'Illegally' Killing Assange: 'A Dead Man Can't Leak Stuff' (VIDEO)," *Huffington Post*, 7 December 2010, archive.today/XiUNo

In early 2014 Brown negotiated a plea deal. At the time of writing he is expected to be sentenced later in 2014. At the end of April 2014, Brown had been detained without trial for one year, seven months, and eighteen

to achieving parity with the dollar.[23] And as early as June, names like "Operation: Empire State Rebellion" and "US Day of Rage" could be heard online, the early reverberations of the popular disenchantment that would by September coalesce into Occupy Wall Street.

The world was ablaze, but the farmlands around Ellingham Hall slept on. Norfolk was an idyllic setting, but my situation

---

days. See "Barrett Brown Signs Plea Deal," Free Barrett Brown website, 3 April 2014, archive.today/SNMda

WikiLeaks released a statement on the persecution of Barrett Brown in September 2013. "Editorial: Release Barrett Brown," WikiLeaks, 16 September 2013, archive.today/lROIX

23. On 5 December 2010, just after VISA, MasterCard, PayPal, Amazon, and other financial companies started denying service to WikiLeaks, a debate broke out on the official web forum for Bitcoin about the risk that donations to WikiLeaks using Bitcoin could provoke unwanted government interest in the then nascent crypto-currency. "Basically, bring it on," wrote one poster. "Satoshi Nakamoto," the pseudonymous inventor of Bitcoin, responded: "No, don't 'bring it on.' The project needs to grow gradually so the software can be strengthened along the way. I make this appeal to WikiLeaks not to try to use Bitcoin. Bitcoin is a small beta community in its infancy. You would not stand to get more than pocket change, and the heat you would bring would likely destroy us at this stage." See the post on the Bitcoin Forum: archive.today/Gvonb#msg26999

Six days later, on 12 December 2010, Satoshi famously vanished from the Bitcoin community, but not before posting this message: "It would have been nice to get this attention in any other context. WikiLeaks has kicked the hornet's nest, and the swarm is headed towards us." See the post on the Bitcoin Forum: archive.today/XuHCD#selection-1803.0-1802.1

WikiLeaks read and agreed with Satoshi's analysis, and decided to put off the launch of a Bitcoin donation channel until the currency had become more established. WikiLeaks' Bitcoin donation address was launched after the currency's first major boom, on 14 June 2011. See the announcement on WikiLeaks' Twitter: archive.today/1hscT

See also the Bitcoin blockchain explorer for WikiLeaks' public donation address: is.gd/wJp3tX

was far from ideal. Pinned there under house arrest, I was at a tactical disadvantage. WikiLeaks had always been a guerilla publisher. We would draw surveillance and censorship in one jurisdiction and redeploy in another, moving across borders like ghosts. But at Ellingham I became an immovable asset under siege. We could no longer choose our battles. Fronts opened up on all sides. I had to learn to think like a general. We were at war.

Our "industrial base" was under bombardment. Whole sections of WikiLeaks' physical and human infrastructure kept disappearing, as the banks placed us under extralegal financial blockades while communications companies, foreign governments, and our human networks were pressured by Washington. Although I had not been charged with a crime, my extradition case ground on through appeal after appeal, swallowing my savings and time and leaving the possibility that at any moment WikiLeaks would be decapitated.[24]

Each month brought news of yet another government task force. So many US and Australian agencies were involved that both countries started to refer to their "whole of government" response in internal documents.[25] The Pentagon's "WikiLeaks War Room"

---

24. For details, see "Extraditing Assange" on the Justice for Assange website: archive.today/6izpC

25. For example, see the announcement by then Australian Attorney General Robert McClelland about WikiLeaks in December 2010: "Doorstop on leaking of US classified documents by WikiLeaks," Attorney-General for Australia website, 29 November 2010, archive.today/Qirks

     The "whole of government" phrasing was still in use in March 2012, as evidenced by the "WikiLeaks Whole of Government Talking Points"

alone had swollen to over a hundred people.[26] A US grand jury was started against us, targeting my staff and me, and is ongoing at the time of writing.[27] The FBI kept raiding our extended human network and attempting to recruit informers. Suddenly, lots of people had "WikiLeaks" on their business cards, but they were not doing business *for* WikiLeaks.

A vast train of sycophants and opportunists were also knocking at my door, surfing the economic gradient created by the conflict, each waiting to grab a moment of proximity and spin it into an expensive tabloid scandal or a favor to be paid.

All we could do was keep our heads down and keep fighting. We rolled out 251,000 US State Department cables, along with thousands of pages of secret files from Guantánamo Bay, to over a hundred countries—a serious logistical, legal, cultural,

memo obtained from the attorney general's office under Freedom of Information: is.gd/MzxG58

Diplomatic cables obtained under Freedom of Information from the Australian Department of Foreign Affairs and Trade also cite private meetings with US officials in referring to the investigation into WikiLeaks as "unprecedented both in its scale and nature," archive.today/OAdui

26. Philip Shenon, "The General Gunning for WikiLeaks," *Daily Beast*, 12 September 2010, archive.today/Onf0m

27. "DOJ Continues Its 'Multi-Subject' Investigation of WikiLeaks," *emptywheel*, 26 April 2014, archive.today/g7zwa

See also Philip Dorling, "Assange targeted by FBI probe, US court documents reveal," *Sydney Morning Herald*, 20 May 2014, archive.today/zFhv7

For the court documents mentioned in the *Sydney Morning Herald* story, see Case 1:12-cv-00127-BJR in the United States District Court for the District of Columbia: is.gd/hvvmgM

For more on the grand jury, see "Background on US v. WikiLeaks," page 205.

and political endeavor.[28] In rare moments of recess—through the prism of a shaky rural internet connection, which kept shutting down in the snow—we kept track of the changes that were afoot and were able to reflect on the meaning of it all. We promised our sources impact and we were delivering. If people were going to prison it would not be for nothing.

* * *

It was into this ferment that Google projected itself that June, touching down in a London airport and making the long drive up into East Anglia to Norfolk and Beccles. Schmidt arrived first, accompanied by his then partner, Lisa Shields. When he introduced her as a vice president of the Council on Foreign Relations—a US foreign-policy think tank with close ties to the State Department—I thought little more of it. Shields herself was straight out of Camelot, having been spotted by John Kennedy Jr.'s side back in the early 1990s. They sat with me and we exchanged pleasantries. They said they had forgotten their dictaphone, so we used mine. We made an agreement that I would forward them the recording and in exchange they would forward me the transcript, to be corrected for accuracy and clarity. We began. Schmidt plunged in at the deep end, straightaway quizzing me on the organizational and technological underpinnings of WikiLeaks.

Some time later Jared Cohen arrived. With him was Scott Malcomson, introduced as the book's editor. Three months after

---

28. "Cablegate," WikiLeaks: www.wikileaks.org/cablegate
"Gitmo Files," WikiLeaks: www.wikileaks.org/gitmo

the meeting Malcomson would enter the State Department as the lead speechwriter and principal advisor to Susan Rice (then US ambassador to the United Nations, now national security advisor). He had previously served as a senior advisor at the United Nations, and is a longtime member of the Council on Foreign Relations. At the time of writing, he is the director of communications at the International Crisis Group.[29]

At this point, the delegation was one part Google, three parts US foreign-policy establishment, but I was still none the wiser. Handshakes out of the way, we got down to business.

Schmidt was a good foil. A late-fiftysomething, squint-eyed behind owlish spectacles, managerially dressed—Schmidt's dour appearance concealed a machinelike analyticity. His questions often skipped to the heart of the matter, betraying a powerful nonverbal structural intelligence. It was the same intellect that had abstracted software-engineering principles to scale Google into a megacorp, ensuring that the corporate infrastructure always met the rate of growth. This was a person who understood how to build and maintain *systems*: systems of information and systems of people. My

---

29. The International Crisis Group bills itself as an "independent, non-profit, non-governmental organization" that works "through field-based analysis and high-level advocacy to prevent and resolve deadly conflict." It has also been described as a "high-level think tank . . . [devised] primarily to provide policy guidance to governments involved in the NATO-led reshaping of the Balkans." See Michael Barker, "Imperial Crusaders For Global Governance," *Swans Commentary*, 20 April 2009, archive.today/b8G3o

Malcomson's International Crisis Group staff profile is available from crisisgroup.org, archive.today/ETYXp

world was new to him, but it was also a world of unfolding human processes, scale, and information flows.

For a man of systematic intelligence, Schmidt's politics—such as I could hear from our discussion—were surprisingly conventional, even banal. He grasped structural relationships quickly, but struggled to verbalize many of them, often shoehorning geopolitical subtleties into Silicon Valley marketese or the ossified State Department microlanguage of his companions.[30] He was at his best when he was speaking (perhaps without realizing it) as an engineer, breaking down complexities into their orthogonal components.

I found Cohen a good listener, but a less interesting thinker, possessed of that relentless conviviality that routinely afflicts career generalists and Rhodes Scholars. As you would expect from his foreign-policy background, Cohen had a knowledge of international flash points and conflicts and moved rapidly between them, detailing different scenarios to test my assertions. But it sometimes felt as if he was riffing on orthodoxies in a way that was designed to impress his former colleagues in official Washington. Malcomson, older, was more pensive, his input thoughtful and generous. Shields was quiet for much of the conversation, taking notes, humoring the bigger egos around the table while she got on with the real work.

As the interviewee I was expected to do most of the talking. I sought to guide them into my worldview. To their credit, I consider the interview perhaps the best I have given. I was out of my comfort zone and I liked it. We ate and then took a walk in the grounds, all

---

30. One might argue that this is living proof of the weak Sapir-Whorf hypothesis. See "Linguistic Relativity," Wikipedia, archive.today/QXJPx

the while on the record. I asked Eric Schmidt to leak US government information requests to WikiLeaks, and he refused, suddenly nervous, citing the illegality of disclosing Patriot Act requests. And then as the evening came on it was done and they were gone, back to the unreal, remote halls of information empire, and I was left to get back to my work. That was the end of it, or so I thought.

* * *

Two months later, WikiLeaks' release of State Department cables was coming to an abrupt end. For three-quarters of a year we had painstakingly managed the publication, pulling in over a hundred global media partners, distributing documents in their regions of influence, and overseeing a worldwide, systematic publication and redaction system, fighting for maximum impact for our sources.

But in an act of gross negligence the *Guardian* newspaper—our former partner—had published the confidential decryption password to all 251,000 cables in a chapter heading in its book, rushed out hastily in February 2011.[31] By mid-August we discovered that a former German employee—whom I had suspended in 2010—was cultivating business relationships with a variety of organizations and individuals by shopping around the location of the encrypted file, paired with the password's whereabouts in the book. At the rate

---

31.　Glenn Greenwald, "Fact and myths in the WikiLeaks/Guardian saga," *Salon*, 2 September 2011, archive.today/5KLJH

　　See also Matt Giuca, "WikiLeaks password leak FAQ," *Unspecified Behaviour*, 3 September 2011, archive.today/ylPUp

　　See also "WikiLeaks: Why the Guardian is wrong and shouldn't have published the password," *Matt's Tumblr*, 1 September 2011, archive.today/aWjj4

the information was spreading, we estimated that within two weeks most intelligence agencies, contractors, and middlemen would have all the cables, but the public would not.

I decided it was necessary to bring forward our publication schedule by four months and contact the State Department to get it on record that we had given them advance warning. The situation would then be harder to spin into another legal or political assault. Unable to raise Louis Susman, then US ambassador to the UK, we tried the front door. WikiLeaks investigations editor Sarah Harrison called the State Department front desk and informed the operator that "Julian Assange" wanted to have a conversation with Hillary Clinton. Predictably, this statement was initially greeted with bureaucratic disbelief. We soon found ourselves in a reenactment of that scene in *Dr. Strangelove*, where Peter Sellers cold-calls the White House to warn of an impending nuclear war and is immediately put on hold. As in the film, we climbed the hierarchy, speaking to incrementally more superior officials until we reached Clinton's senior legal advisor. He told us he would call us back. We hung up, and waited.

When the phone rang half an hour later, it was not the State Department on the other end of the line. Instead, it was Joseph Farrell, the WikiLeaks staffer who had set up the meeting with Google. He had just received an email from Lisa Shields seeking to confirm that it was indeed WikiLeaks calling the State Department.

It was at this point that I realized Eric Schmidt might not have been an emissary of Google alone. Whether officially or not, he had been keeping some company that placed him very close to Washington, DC, including a well-documented relationship with President Obama. Not only had Hillary Clinton's people known that Eric Schmidt's partner had visited me, but they had also elected to use her as a back channel. While WikiLeaks had been deeply involved in publishing the inner archive of the US State Department, the US State Department had, in effect, snuck into the WikiLeaks command center and hit me up for a free lunch. Two years later, in the wake of his early 2013 visits to China, North Korea, and Burma, it would come to be appreciated that the chairman of Google might be conducting, in one way or another, "back-channel diplomacy" for Washington. But at the time it was a novel thought.[32]

I put it aside until February 2012, when WikiLeaks—along with over thirty of our international media partners—began publishing the Global Intelligence Files: the internal email spool from the Texas-based private intelligence firm Stratfor.[33] One of our stronger investigative partners—the Beirut-based newspaper *Al Akhbar*—scoured the emails for intelligence on Jared Cohen.[34] The people at Stratfor, who liked to think of themselves as a sort of corporate CIA, were acutely conscious of other ventures that they perceived as making inroads into their sector. Google had turned up on their radar. In a series of colorful emails they discussed a pattern of activity conducted by Cohen under the Google Ideas aegis, suggesting what the "do" in "think/do tank" actually means.

---

32. Andrew Jacobs, "Visit by Google Chairman May Benefit North Korea," *New York Times*, 10 January 2013, archive.today/bXrQ2

33. Jeremy Hammond, a brave and principled young digital revolutionary, was later accused by the US government of ferreting these documents out and giving them to WikiLeaks. He is now a political prisoner in the US, sentenced to ten years after speaking to an FBI informer.

34. Yazan al-Saadi, "StratforLeaks: Google Ideas Director Involved in 'Regime Change,'" *Al Akhbar*, 14 March 2012, archive.today/gHMzq

Cohen's directorate appeared to cross over from public relations and "corporate responsibility" work into active corporate intervention in foreign affairs at a level that is normally reserved for states. Jared Cohen could be wryly named Google's "director of regime change." According to the emails, he was trying to plant his fingerprints on some of the major historical events in the contemporary Middle East. He could be placed in Egypt during the revolution, meeting with Wael Ghonim, the Google employee whose arrest and imprisonment hours later would make him a PR-friendly symbol of the uprising in the Western press. Meetings had been planned in Palestine and Turkey, both of which—claimed Stratfor emails—were killed by the senior Google leadership as too risky. Only a few months before he met with me, Cohen was planning a trip to the edge of Iran in Azerbaijan to "engage the Iranian communities closer to the border," as part of Google Ideas' project on "repressive societies." In internal emails Stratfor's vice president for intelligence, Fred Burton (himself a former State Department security official), wrote:

> Google is getting WH [White House] and State Dept support and air cover. In reality they are doing things the CIA cannot do . . . [Cohen] is going to get himself kidnapped or killed. Might be the best thing to happen to expose Google's covert role in foaming up-risings, to be blunt. The US Gov't can then disavow knowledge and Google is left holding the shit-bag.[35]

---

35. "Re: GOOGLE & Iran ** internal use only—pls do not forward **," email ID 1121800 (27 February 2011), Global Intelligence Files, WikiLeaks, 14 March 2012, archive.today/sjxuG

In further internal communication, Burton said his sources on Cohen's activities were Marty Lev—Google's director of security and safety—and Eric Schmidt himself.[36]

For more internal Stratfor discussions about Jared Cohen and Google, see:

"Egypt - Google ** Suggest you read," email ID 1122191 (9 February 2011), Global Intelligence Files, WikiLeaks, 14 March 2012, archive.today/DCzlA

"Re: More on Cohen," email ID 1629270 (9 February 2011), Global Intelligence Files, WikiLeaks, 14 March 2012, archive.today/opQ3a

"Re: Google Shitstorm Moving to Gaza (internal use only)," email ID 1111729 (10 February 2011), Global Intelligence Files, WikiLeaks, 14 March 2012, archive.today/vpK3F

"Re: Google's Cohen Activist Role," email ID 1123044 (10 February 2011), Global Intelligence Files, WikiLeaks, 11 March 2013, archive.today/nvFP6

"Re: movements.org founder Cohen," email ID 1113596 (11 February 2011), Global Intelligence Files, WikiLeaks, 6 March 2012, archive.today/ToYjC

"Re: discussion: who is next?," email ID 1113965 (11 February 2011), Global Intelligence Files, WikiLeaks, 14 March 2012, archive.today/ofBMr

"GOOGLE Loose Canon Bound for Turkey & UAE (SENSITIVE - DO NOT FORWARD)," email ID 1164190 (10 March 2011), Global Intelligence Files, WikiLeaks, 14 March 2012, archive.today/Jpy4F

"Re: [alpha] GOOGLE - Cohen & Hosting of Terrorists," email ID 1133861 (22 March 2011), Global Intelligence Files, WikiLeaks, 14 March 2012, archive.today/OCR78

"[alpha] Jared Cohen (GOOGLE)," email ID 1160182 (30 March 2011), Global Intelligence Files, WikiLeaks, 14 March 2012, archive.today/FYQYe

For these emails and more, see the collection of sources at when.google.met.wikileaks.org

36. "Re: GOOGLE's Jared Cohen update," email ID 398679 (14 February 2011), Global Intelligence Files, WikiLeaks, 14 March 2012, archive.today/IoFw4

Looking for something more concrete, I began to search in WikiLeaks' archive for information on Cohen. State Department cables released as part of Cablegate reveal that Cohen had been in Afghanistan in 2009, trying to convince the four major Afghan mobile phone companies to move their antennas onto US military bases.[37] In Lebanon he quietly worked to establish an intellectual and clerical rival to Hezbollah, the "Higher Shia League."[38] And in London he offered Bollywood movie executives funds to insert anti-extremist content into their films, and promised to connect them to related networks in Hollywood.[39]

This email is included in the collection of sources at: when.google.met.wikileaks.org

37. "Using connection technologies to promote US strategic interests in Afghanistan: mobile banking, telecommunications insurance, and co-location of cell phone towers," canonical ID: 09KABUL2020_a, Public Library of US Diplomacy, WikiLeaks, archive.today/loAlC

This cable is included in the collection of sources at: when.google.met.wikileaks.org

In May 2014, WikiLeaks revealed that the NSA had gained access to all Afghan mobile phone calls and was recording all of them for later retrieval. See "WikiLeaks statement on the mass recording of Afghan telephone calls by the NSA," WikiLeaks, 23 May 2014, archive.today/lp6Pl

38. From the Public Library of US Diplomacy, WikiLeaks, see cables with canonical IDs: 07BEIRUT1944_a, 08BEIRUT910_a, 08BEIRUT912_a, 08BEIRUT918_a, 08BEIRUT919_a, 08BEIRUT1389_a, and 09BEIRUT234_a. Collection available at: archive.today/34MyI

See also the collection of sources at when.google.met.wikileaks.org

39. "EUR senior advisor Pandith and s/p advisor Cohen's visit to the UK, October 9-14, 2007," canonical ID: 07LONDON4045_a, Public Library of US Diplomacy, WikiLeaks, archive.today/mxXGQ

For more on Jared Cohen from the WikiLeaks archives see: archive.today/5fVm2

See also the collection of sources at when.google.met.wikileaks.org

Three days after he visited me at Ellingham Hall, Jared Cohen flew to Ireland to direct the "Save Summit," an event cosponsored by Google Ideas and the Council on Foreign Relations. Gathering former inner-city gang members, right-wing militants, violent nationalists, and "religious extremists" from all over the world together in one place, the event aimed to workshop technological solutions to the problem of "violent extremism."[40] What could go wrong?

Cohen's world seems to be one event like this after another: endless soirees for the cross-fertilization of influence between elites and their vassals, under the pious rubric of "civil society." The received wisdom in advanced capitalist societies is that there still exists an organic "civil society sector" in which institutions form autonomously and come together to manifest the interests and will of citizens. The fable has it that the boundaries of this sector are respected by actors from government and the "private sector," leaving a safe space for NGOs and nonprofits to advocate for things like human rights, free speech, and accountable government.

This sounds like a great idea. But if it was ever true, it has not been for decades. Since at least the 1970s, authentic actors like unions and churches have folded under a sustained assault by free-market statism, transforming "civil society" into a buyer's market for political factions and corporate interests looking to exert influence at arm's length. The last forty years have seen a huge proliferation of think tanks and political NGOs whose purpose, beneath all the verbiage, is to execute political agendas by proxy.

---

40. See "Summit Against Violent Extremism (SAVE)" on the Council on Foreign Relations website, archive.today/rA1tA

It is not just obvious neocon front groups like Foreign Policy Initiative.[41] It also includes fatuous Western NGOs like Freedom House, where naïve but well-meaning career nonprofit workers are twisted in knots by political funding streams, denouncing non-Western human rights violations while keeping local abuses firmly in their blind spots. The civil society conference circuit—which flies developing-world activists across the globe hundreds of times a year to bless the unholy union between "government and private stakeholders" at geopoliticized events like the "Stockholm Internet Forum"—simply could not exist if it were not blasted with millions of dollars in political funding annually.

Scan the memberships of the biggest US think tanks and institutes and the same names keep cropping up. Cohen's Save Summit went on to seed AVE, or AgainstViolentExtremism.org, a long-term project whose principal backer besides Google Ideas is the Gen Next Foundation. This foundation's website says it is an "exclusive membership organization and platform for successful individuals" that aims to bring about "social change" driven by venture capital funding.[42] Gen Next's "private sector and non-profit foundation support avoids some of the potential perceived conflicts of interest faced by initiatives funded by governments."[43] Jared Cohen is an executive member.

---

41. For an insight into Foreign Policy Initiative, see Max Blumenthal, Rania Khalek, "How Cold War–Hungry Neocons Stage Managed RT Anchor Liz Wahl's Resignation," *Truthdig*, 19 March 2014, archive.today/JSUHq

42. "About GNF," Gen Next Foundation website, archive.today/p91bd

43. "AgainstViolentExtremism.org," Gen Next Foundation website: archive.today/Rhdtf

Gen Next also backs an NGO, launched by Cohen toward the end of his State Department tenure, for bringing internet-based global "pro-democracy activists" into the US foreign relations patronage network.[44] The group originated as the "Alliance of Youth Movements" with an inaugural summit in New York City in 2008 funded by the State Department and encrusted with the logos of corporate sponsors.[45] The summit flew in carefully selected social media activists from "problem areas" like Venezuela and Cuba to watch speeches by the Obama campaign's new-media team and the State Department's James Glassman, and to network with public relations consultants, "philanthropists," and US media personalities.[46]

---

44. "Movements.org," Gen Next Foundation website, archive.today/oVlqH

Note this extract from a confidential report of a March 2011 meeting between Stratfor and the "main organizer" of Movements.org: "How Movements.org got started: [This part is not for publication] in 2008 it became apparent to the USG that they needed to do public diplomacy over the internet. So Jared Cohen was at DoS then and played a major role in starting the organization. The main goal was just spreading the good word about the US." "[alpha] INSIGHT- US/MENA- Movements. org," email ID 1356429 (29 March 2011), Global Intelligence Files, WikiLeaks, 4 March 2013, archive.today/PgQji

See also the collection of sources at when.google.met.wikileaks.org

45. For more on this event see Joseph L. Flatley, "Being cynical: Julian Assange, Eric Schmidt, and the year's weirdest book," *Verge*, 7 June 2013, archive.today/gfLEr

See also "The Summit: New York City, The 2008 Inaugural Alliance of Youth Movements Summit," Movements.org website, archive.today/H2Ox1#2008

See the logos of the corporate sponsors at "About movements.org," Movements.org website, archive.today/DQo19

46. "Attendee Biographies, 3-5 December 2008, New York City," Alliance of Youth Movements, is.gd/bLOVxT

The outfit held two more invite-only summits in London and Mexico City where the delegates were directly addressed via video link by Hillary Clinton:[47]

> You are the vanguard of a rising generation of citizen activists. . . . And that makes you the kind of leaders we need.[48]

In 2011, the Alliance of Youth Movements rebranded as "Movements.org." In 2012 Movements.org became a division of "Advancing Human Rights," a new NGO set up by Robert L. Bernstein after he resigned from Human Rights Watch (which he had originally founded) because he felt it should not cover Israeli and US human rights abuses.[49] Advancing Human Rights aims to right Human Rights Watch's wrong by focusing exclusively on "dictatorships."[50]

See also "09 Summit, Attendee Biographies, 14-16 October 2009, Mexico City," Alliance of Youth Movements, is.gd/MddXp7

See also "Attendee Biographies, 9-11 March 2010, London," Movements.org, is.gd/dHTVit

47. "The Summit: London, The 2010 Alliance For Youth Movements Summit," Movements.org website, archive.today/H2Ox1#2010

And "The Summit: Mexico City, The 2009 Alliance of Youth Movements Summit," Movements.org website, archive.today/H2Ox1#2009

48. Hillary Rodham Clinton, "Secretary Clinton's Video Message for Alliance of Youth Movements Summit," US Department of State, 16 October 2009, archive.today/I2x6U

See also Hillary Rodham Clinton, "Remarks At TecMilenio University," US Department of State, 26 March 2009, archive.today/49ACj

49. Scott Shane, "Groups to Help Online Activists in Authoritarian Countries," *New York Times*, 11 June 2012, archive.today/jqq9U

50. "Mission Statement," Advancing Human Rights website: archive.today/kBzYe

Cohen stated that the merger of his Movements.org outfit with Advancing Human Rights was "irresistible," pointing to the latter's "phenomenal network of cyberactivists in the Middle East and North Africa."[51] He then joined the Advancing Human Rights board, which also includes Richard Kemp, the former commander of British forces in occupied Afghanistan.[52] In its present guise, Movements.org continues to receive funding from Gen Next, as well as from Google, MSNBC, and PR giant Edelman, which represents General Electric, Boeing, and Shell, among others.[53]

Google Ideas is bigger, but it follows the same game plan. Glance down the speaker lists of its annual invite-only get-togethers, such as "Crisis in a Connected World" in October 2013. Social network theorists and activists give the event a veneer of authenticity,

---

Scott Shane, "Groups to Help Online Activists in Authoritarian Countries," *New York Times*, 11 June 2012, archive.today/jqq9U

51. Ibid.

52. "People," Advancing Human Rights website, archive.today/pXmPk

53. Edelman is famous for a series of astroturfing campaigns for Big Tobacco and Walmart. The sourcewatch.org page on Edelman, which is worth reading in full, has a section on Edelman's strategy toward co-opting the nongovernmental sector: "Edelman PR tells clients that activists are winning because 'they play offense all the time; they take their message to the consumer; they are ingenious at building coalitions; they always have a clear agenda; they move at Internet speed; they speak in the media's tone.' The solution, it argues, are partnerships between NGOs and business. 'Our experience to date is positive,' they say, citing examples such as 'Chiquita-Rainforest Alliance' and 'Home Depot-Forest Stewardship Council.'" See "Daniel J. Edelman, Inc.," SourceWatch website, archive.today/APbOf

For the sponsors of Movements.org, see "About movements.org," Movements.org website, archive.today/NMkOy

but in truth it boasts a toxic piñata of attendees: US officials, telecom magnates, security consultants, finance capitalists, and foreign-policy tech vultures like Alec Ross (Cohen's twin at the State Department).[54] At the hard core are the arms contractors and career military: active US Cyber Command chieftains, and even the admiral responsible for all US military operations in Latin America from 2006 to 2009. Tying up the package are Jared Cohen and the chairman of Google, Eric Schmidt.[55]

I began to think of Schmidt as a brilliant but politically hapless Californian tech billionaire who had been exploited by the very US foreign-policy types he had collected to act as translators between himself and official Washington—a West Coast–East Coast illustration of the principal-agent dilemma.[56]

I was wrong.

* * *

Eric Schmidt was born in Washington, DC, where his father had worked as a professor and economist for the Nixon Treasury. He attended high school in Arlington, Virginia, before graduating with

---

54. For an example of Alec Ross's writing, see Alec Ross, Ben Scott, "Social media: power to the people?" *NATO Review*, 2011, archive.today/L6sb3

55. "Speakers," Conflict in a Connected World website, archive.today/Ed8rA

56. The "principal-agent problem" or "agency dilemma" is where the initiating party, the principal, tasks an accepting party, the agent, to act on his or her behalf, but where the interests of the two parties are not sufficiently aligned and the agent uses his or her position to exploit the principal. A lawyer who makes decisions that are in the lawyer's, but not the client's, interests is a classic example.

a degree in engineering from Princeton. In 1979 Schmidt headed out West to Berkeley, where he received his PhD before joining Stanford/ Berkley spin-off Sun Microsystems in 1983. By the time he left Sun, sixteen years later, he had become part of its executive leadership.

Sun had significant contracts with the US government, but it was not until he was in Utah as CEO of Novell that records show Schmidt strategically engaging Washington's overt political class. Federal campaign finance records show that on January 6, 1999, Schmidt donated two lots of $1,000 to the Republican senator for Utah, Orrin Hatch. On the same day Schmidt's wife, Wendy, is also listed giving two lots of $1,000 to Senator Hatch. By the start of 2001 over a dozen other politicians and PACs, including Al Gore, George W. Bush, Dianne Feinstein, and Hillary Clinton, were on the Schmidts' payroll, in one case for $100,000.[57] By 2013, Eric Schmidt— who had become publicly over-associated with the Obama White House—was more politic. Eight Republicans and eight Democrats were directly funded, as were two PACs. That April, $32,300 went to the National Republican Senatorial Committee. A month later the same amount, $32,300, headed off to the Democratic Senatorial Campaign Committee. Why Schmidt was donating exactly the same amount of money to both parties is a $64,600 question.[58]

---

57. "PAC" stands for "Political Action Committee," a campaign-funding pool often used to obscure support for particular politicians, to sidestep campaign-finance regulations, or to campaign on a particular issue.

58. All political donation figures sourced from OpenSecrets.org (opensecrets. org/indivs) and the US Federal Election Commission (fec.gov/finance/ disclosure/norindsea.shtml). See the results listed for Eric Schmidt on the Federal Election Commission website, archive.today/yjXoi

It was also in 1999 that Schmidt joined the board of a Washington, DC–based group: the New America Foundation, a merger of well-connected centrist forces (in DC terms). The foundation and its 100 staff serve as an influence mill, using its network of approved national security, foreign policy, and technology pundits to place hundreds of articles and op-eds per year. By 2008 Schmidt had become chairman of its board of directors. As of 2013 the New America Foundation's principal funders (each contributing over $1 million) are listed as Eric and Wendy Schmidt, the US State Department, and the Bill & Melinda Gates Foundation. Secondary funders include Google, USAID, and Radio Free Asia.[59]

Schmidt's involvement in the New America Foundation places him firmly in the Washington establishment nexus. The foundation's other board members, seven of whom also list themselves as members of the Council on Foreign Relations, include Francis Fukuyama, one of the intellectual fathers of the neoconservative movement; Rita Hauser, who served on the President's Intelligence Advisory Board under both Bush and Obama; Jonathan Soros, the son of George Soros; Walter Russell Mead, a US security strategist and editor of the *American Interest*; Helene Gayle, who sits on the boards of Coca-Cola, Colgate-Palmolive, the Rockefeller Foundation, the State Department's Foreign Affairs Policy Unit, the Council on Foreign Relations, the Center for Strategic and International Studies, the White House Fellows program, and Bono's ONE Campaign; and Daniel Yergin, oil geostrategist, former chair of the US Department of Energy's Task

---

See also a screenshot of the results listed for Eric and Wendy Schmidt on the OpenSecrets.org website, archive.today/o6hiB

59.   "Our Funding," New America Foundation website, archive.today/3FnFm

Force on Strategic Energy Research, and author of *The Prize: The Epic Quest for Oil, Money and Power*.[60]

The chief executive of the foundation, appointed in 2013, is Jared Cohen's former boss at the State Department's Policy Planning Staff, Anne-Marie Slaughter, a Princeton law and international relations wonk with an eye for revolving doors.[61] She is everywhere at the time of writing, issuing calls for Obama to respond to the Ukraine crisis not only by deploying covert US forces into the country but also by dropping bombs on Syria—on the basis that this will send a message to Russia and China.[62] Along with Schmidt, she is a 2013 attendee of

---

60. Francis Fukuyama profile on the New America Foundation website: archive.today/6ZKk5

    Rita E. Hauser profile on the New America Foundation website: archive.today/oAvJf

    Jonathan Soros profile on the New America Foundation website: archive.today/lTJy9

    Walter Russell Mead profile on the New America Foundation website: archive.today/APejM

    Helene D. Gayle profile on the New America Foundation website: archive.today/72plM

    Daniel Yergin profile on the New America Foundation website: archive.today/kQ4ys

    See the full board of directors on the New America Foundation website: archive.today/iBvgl

61. Anne-Marie Slaughter profile on the New America Foundation website: archive.today/yIoLP

62. "The solution to the crisis in Ukraine lies in part in Syria. It is time for US President Barack Obama to demonstrate that he can order the offensive use of force in circumstances other than secret drone attacks or covert operations. The result will change the strategic calculus not only in Damascus, but also in Moscow, not to mention Beijing and Tokyo." Anne-Marie Slaughter, "Stopping Russia Starts in Syria," *Project Syndicate*, 23 April 2014, archive.today/GiLng

the Bilderberg conference and sits on the State Department's Foreign Affairs Policy Board.[63]

There was nothing politically hapless about Eric Schmidt. I had been too eager to see a politically unambitious Silicon Valley engineer, a relic of the good old days of computer science graduate culture on the West Coast. But that is not the sort of person who attends the Bilderberg conference four years running, who pays regular visits to the White House, or who delivers "fireside chats" at the World Economic Forum in Davos.[64] Schmidt's emergence

---

Jared Cohen has retweeted approval for Slaughter on the issue. For example, he shared a supportive tweet on 26 April 2014 that claimed that the argument in the article quoted above was "spot on." archive.today/qLyxo

63. On the Bilderberg conference see Matthew Holehouse, "Bilderberg Group 2013: guest list and agenda," *Telegraph*, 6 June 2013, archive.today/PeJGc

On the State Department's Foreign Affairs Policy Board, see the list of current board members on the US Department of State website: archive.today/Why8v

64. Attendee lists for Bilderberg conferences since 2010 are available from the Bilderberg website: www.bilderbergmeetings.org Eric Schmidt was photographed at Bilderberg 2014 in Copenhagen, meeting with Viviane Reding, the EU Commissioner for Justice, and Alex Karp, the CEO of Palantir Technologies, an intelligence data-mining company which sells search and data integration services to clients in the US law enforcement and intelligence community, and which was launched with funding from the CIA's venture capital fund, In-Q-Tel. See Charlie Skelton, "Bilderberg conference 2014: eating our politicians for breakfast," *Guardian*, 30 May 2014, archive.today/pUY5b

In 2011, Palantir was involved in the HBGary scandal, having been exposed as part of a group of contractors proposing to take down WikiLeaks. For more on this, see "Background on US v. WikiLeaks," page 205. See also Andy Greenberg, Ryan Mac,

as Google's "foreign minister"—making pomp and ceremony state visits across geopolitical fault lines—had not come out of nowhere; it had been presaged by years of assimilation within US establishment networks of reputation and influence.

On a personal level, Schmidt and Cohen are perfectly likable people. But Google's chairman is a classic "head of industry" player, with all of the ideological baggage that comes with that role.[65] Schmidt fits exactly where he is: the point where the centrist, liberal, and imperialist tendencies meet in American political life. By all appearances, Google's bosses genuinely believe in the civilizing power of enlightened multinational corporations, and they see this mission as continuous with the shaping of the world according to the better judgment of the "benevolent superpower." They will tell you that open-mindedness is a virtue, but all perspectives that challenge the exceptionalist drive at the heart of American foreign policy will remain invisible to them. This is the impenetrable banality of "don't be evil." They believe that they are doing good. And that is a problem.

* * *

"How A 'Deviant' Philosopher Built Palantir, A CIA-Funded Data-Mining Juggernaut," *Forbes*, 2 September 2013, archive.today/ozAZ8

White House visitor records are available from its website, archive.today/QFQx0

For coverage of Schmidt at the World Economic Forum see Emily Young, "Davos 2014: Google's Schmidt warning on jobs," BBC, 23 January 2014, archive.today/jGl7B

See also Larry Elliott, "Davos debates income inequality but still invites tax avoiders," *Guardian*, 19 January 2014, archive.today/IR767

65. Adrianne Jeffries, "Google's Eric Schmidt: 'let us celebrate capitalism,'" *Verge*, 7 March 2014, archive.today/gZepE

Google is different. Google is visionary. Google is the future. Google is more than just a company. Google gives back to the community. Google is a force for good.

Even when Google airs its corporate ambivalence publicly, it does little to dislodge these items of faith.[66] The company's reputation is seemingly unassailable. Google's colorful, playful logo is imprinted on human retinas just under six billion times each day, 2.1 trillion times a year—an opportunity for respondent conditioning enjoyed by no other company in history.[67] Caught red-handed last year making petabytes of personal data available to the US intelligence community through the PRISM program, Google nevertheless continues to coast on the goodwill generated by its "don't be evil" doublespeak. A few symbolic open letters to the White House later and it seems all is forgiven. Even anti-surveillance campaigners cannot help themselves, at once condemning government spying but trying to alter Google's invasive surveillance practices using appeasement strategies.[68]

---

66. For an example of Google's corporate ambivalence on the issue of privacy see Richard Esguerra, "Google CEO Eric Schmidt Dismisses the Importance of Privacy," Electronic Frontier Foundation, 10 December 2009, archive.today/rwyQ7

67. Figures correct as of 2013. See "Google Annual Search Statistics," Statistic Brain (Statistic Brain Research Institute), 1 January 2014, archive.today/W7DgX

68. There is an uncomfortable willingness among privacy campaigners to discriminate against mass surveillance conducted by the state to the exclusion of similar surveillance conducted for profit by large corporations. Partially, this is a vestigial ethic from the Californian libertarian origins of online pro-privacy campaigning. Partially, it is a symptom of the superior public relations enjoyed by Silicon Valley technology corporations, and

Nobody wants to acknowledge that Google has grown big and bad. But it has. Schmidt's tenure as CEO saw Google integrate with the shadiest of US power structures as it expanded into a geographically invasive megacorporation. But Google has always been comfortable with this proximity. Long before company founders Larry Page and Sergey Brin hired Schmidt in 2001, their initial research upon which Google was based had been partly funded by the

---

the fact that those corporations also provide the bulk of private funding for the flagship digital privacy advocacy groups, leading to a conflict of interest.

At the individual level, many of even the most committed privacy campaigners have an unacknowledged addiction to easy-to-use, privacy-destroying amenities like Gmail, Facebook, and Apple products. As a result, privacy campaigners frequently overlook corporate surveillance abuses. When they do address the abuses of companies like Google, campaigners tend to appeal to the logic of the market, urging companies to make small concessions to user privacy in order to repair their approval ratings. There is the false assumption that market forces ensure that Silicon Valley is a natural government antagonist, and that it wants to be on the public's side—that profit-driven multinational corporations partake more of the spirit of democracy than government agencies.

Many privacy advocates justify a predominant focus on abuses by the state on the basis that the state enjoys a monopoly on coercive force. For example, Edward Snowden was reported to have said that tech companies do not "put warheads on foreheads." See Barton Gellman, "Edward Snowden, after months of NSA revelations, says his mission's accomplished," *Washington Post*, 23 December 2013, archive.today/d6P8q

This view downplays the fact that powerful corporations are part of the nexus of power around the state, and that they enjoy the ability to deploy its coercive power, just as the state often exerts its influence through the agency of powerful corporations. The movement to abolish privacy is twin-horned. Privacy advocates who focus exclusively on one of those horns will find themselves gored on the other.

Defense Advanced Research Projects Agency (DARPA).[69] And even as Schmidt's Google developed an image as the overly friendly giant of global tech, it was building a close relationship with the intelligence community.

In 2003 the US National Security Agency (NSA) had already started systematically violating the Foreign Intelligence Surveillance Act (FISA) under its director General Michael Hayden.[70] These were the days of the "Total Information Awareness" program.[71] Before PRISM was ever dreamed of, under orders from the Bush

---

69. See section 7, Acknowledgments, in *The Anatomy of a Large-Scale Hypertextual Web Search Engine*, Sergey Brin, Lawrence Page (Computer Science Department, Stanford University, 1998): "The research described here was conducted as part of the Stanford Integrated Digital Library Project, supported by the National Science Foundation under Cooperative Agreement IRI-9411306. Funding for this cooperative agreement is also provided by DARPA and NASA, and by Interval Research, and the industrial partners of the Stanford Digital Libraries Project," archive.today/tb5VL

70. Michael Hayden is now with the Chertoff Group, a consultancy firm which describes itself as a "premier security and risk management advisory firm." It was founded and is chaired by Michael Chertoff, who was the former secretary of the Department of Homeland Security under President George W. Bush. See Marcus Baram, "Fear Pays: Chertoff, Ex-Security Officials Slammed For Cashing In On Government Experience," *Huffington Post*, 23 November 2010, updated 25 May 2011, archive.today/iaM1b

71. "Total Information Awareness" was a radical post-9/11 US intelligence program under the Defense Advanced Research Projects Agency to surveil and gather detailed information about individuals in order to anticipate their behavior. The program was officially discontinued in 2003 after public outcry, but its legacy can arguably be seen in recent disclosures on bulk spying by the National Security Agency. See Shane Harris, "Giving In to the Surveillance State," *New York Times*, 22 August 2012, archive.today/v4zNm

White House the NSA was already aiming to "collect it all, sniff it all, know it all, process it all, exploit it all."[72] During the same period, Google—whose publicly declared corporate mission is to collect and "organize the world's information and make it universally accessible and useful"[73]—was accepting NSA money to the tune of $2 million to provide the agency with search tools for its rapidly accreting hoard of stolen knowledge.[74]

In 2004, after taking over Keyhole, a mapping tech startup cofounded by the National Geospatial-Intelligence Agency (NGA) and the CIA, Google developed the technology into Google Maps, an enterprise version of which it has since shopped to the Pentagon and associated federal and state agencies on multimillion-dollar

---

72. "The Munk Debate on State Surveillance: Edward Snowden Video" (video), Munk Debates, archive.today/zOj0t

    See also Jane Mayer, "The Secret Sharer: Is Thomas Drake an enemy of the state?" *New Yorker*, 23 May 2011, archive.today/pXoy9

73. "Company overview," Google company website, archive.today/JavDC

74. *Lost in the Cloud: Google and the US Government* (report), Consumer Watchdog's Inside Google, January 2011, bit.ly/1qNoHQ9

    See also Verne Kopytoff, "Google has lots to do with intelligence," *San Francisco Chronicle*, 30 March 2008, archive.today/VNEJi

    See also Yasha Levine, "Oakland emails give another glimpse into the Google-Military-Surveillance Complex," *Pando Daily*, 7 March 2014, archive.today/W35WU

    See also Yasha Levine, "Emails showing Google's closeness with the NSA Director really aren't that surprising," *Pando Daily*, 13 May 2014, archive.today/GRT18

    Yasha Levine has written a number of investigative articles on Google's ties to the military and intelligence industry. My discussion of these ties draws on Levine's research, which is worth reading in the original at: pando.com/author/ylevine

contracts.[75] In 2008, Google helped launch an NGA spy satellite, the GeoEye-1, into space. Google shares the photographs from the satellite with the US military and intelligence communities.[76] In 2010, NGA awarded Google a $27 million contract for "geospatial visualization services."[77]

In 2010, after the Chinese government was accused of hacking Google, the company entered into a "formal information-sharing" relationship with the NSA, which was said to allow NSA analysts to "evaluate vulnerabilities" in Google's hardware and software.[78] Although the exact contours of the deal have never been disclosed, the NSA brought in other government agencies to help, including the FBI and the Department of Homeland Security.

Around the same time, Google was becoming involved in a program known as the "Enduring Security Framework"[79] (ESF), which entailed the sharing of information between Silicon

---

75. Yasha Levine, "Oakland emails give another glimpse into the Google-Military-Surveillance Complex," *Pando Daily*, 7 March 2014, archive.today/W35WU

    For more on Google's ties to the CIA, see Noah Shachtman, "Exclusive: Google, CIA Invest in 'Future' of Web Monitoring," *Wired*, 28 July 2010, archive.today/e0LNL

76. Yasha Levine, "Oakland emails give another glimpse into the Google-Military-Surveillance Complex," *Pando Daily*, 7 March 2014, archive.today/W35WU

77. Ibid.

78. Ellen Nakashima, "Google to enlist NSA to help it ward off cyberattacks," *Washington Post*, 4 February 2010, archive.today/hVTVl

79. The official name for US military occupation of Afghanistan is similar: "Operation Enduring Freedom." See "Infinite Justice, out—Enduring Freedom, in," BBC, 25 September 2001, archive.today/f0fp7

Valley tech companies and Pentagon-affiliated agencies "at network speed."[80] Emails obtained in 2014 under Freedom of Information requests show Schmidt and his fellow Googler Sergey Brin corresponding on first-name terms with NSA chief General Keith Alexander about ESF.[81] Reportage on the emails focused on the familiarity in the correspondence: "General Keith . . . so great to see you . . . !" Schmidt wrote. But most reports overlooked a crucial detail. "Your insights as a key member of the Defense Industrial Base," Alexander wrote to Brin, "are valuable to ensure ESF's efforts have measurable impact."

The Department of Homeland Security defines the Defense Industrial Base as "the worldwide industrial complex that enables research and development, as well as design, production, delivery, and maintenance of military weapons systems, subsystems, and components or parts, *to meet U.S. military requirements* [emphasis added]."[82] The Defense Industrial Base provides "products and services that are essential to mobilize, deploy, and sustain military operations." Does it include regular commercial services purchased by the US military? No. The definition specifically excludes the purchase of regular commercial services. Whatever makes Google a "key member of the Defense Industrial Base," it is not recruitment campaigns pushed out through Google AdWords or soldiers checking their Gmail.

---

80. Jason Leopold, "Exclusive: emails reveal close Google relationship with NSA," *Al Jazeera America*, 6 May 2014, archive.today/V0fdG

81. Ibid.

82. "Defense Industrial Base Sector," on the US Homeland Security website: archive.today/Y7Z23

In 2012, Google arrived on the list of top-spending Washington, DC, lobbyists—a list typically stalked exclusively by the US Chamber of Commerce, military contractors, and the petrocarbon leviathans.[83] Google entered the rankings above military aerospace giant Lockheed Martin, with a total of $18.2 million spent in 2012 to Lockheed's $15.3 million. Boeing, the military contractor that absorbed McDonnell Douglas in 1997, also came below Google, at $15.6 million spent, as did Northrop Grumman at $17.5 million.

In autumn 2013 the Obama administration was trying to drum up support for US airstrikes against Syria. Despite setbacks, the administration continued to press for military action well into September with speeches and public announcements by both President Obama and Secretary of State John Kerry.[84] On September 10, Google lent its front page—the most popular on the internet—to the war effort, inserting a line below the search box reading "Live! Secretary Kerry answers questions on Syria. Today via Hangout at 2pm ET."[85]

---

83. See "Top Spenders" under "Influence and Lobbying" on the OpenSecrets.org website: archive.today/xQyui
    See also Tom Hamburger, "Google, once disdainful of lobbying, now a master of Washington influence," *Washington Post*, 13 April 2014, archive.today/oil7k

84. Sy Hersh has written two articles about the Obama administration's ill-fated case for "intervention" in Syria. See Seymour M. Hersh, "Whose Sarin?" *London Review of Books*, 19 December 2013, archive.today/THPGh
    See also Seymour M. Hersh, "The Red Line and the Rat Line," *London Review of Books*, 17 April 2014, archive.today/qp5jB

85. An archive snapshot of the page can be found at archive.today/Q6uq8 Google explicitly prides itself on keeping its front page free of all

As the self-described "radical centrist"[86] *New York Times* columnist Tom Friedman wrote in 1999, sometimes it is not enough to leave the global dominance of American tech corporations to something as mercurial as "the free market":

> The hidden hand of the market will never work without a hidden fist. McDonald's cannot flourish without McDonnell Douglas, the designer of the F-15. And the hidden fist that keeps the world safe for Silicon Valley's technologies to flourish is called the US Army, Air Force, Navy and Marine Corps.[87]

If anything has changed since those words were written, it is that Silicon Valley has grown restless with that passive role, aspiring

---

interference. Its purity and sacredness are incorporated into Google's corporate manifesto: "Our homepage interface is clear and simple, and pages load instantly. Placement in search results is never sold to anyone, and advertising is not only clearly marked as such, it offers relevant content and is not distracting." See "Ten things we know to be true," Google company website, archive.today/s7v9B#selection-243.52-243.277

On the rare occasions Google adds a single line to the search page to plug its own projects, like the Chrome browser, that choice itself becomes news. See Cade Metz, "Google smears Chrome on 'sacred' home page," *Register*, 9 September 2008, archive.today/kfneV

See also Hayley Tsukayama, "Google advertises Nexus 7 on home page," *Washington Post*, 28 August 2012, archive.today/QYfBV

86. Thomas Friedman has published several columns extolling the virtues of his "radical centrism," such as "Make Way for the Radical Center," *New York Times*, 23 July 2011, archive.today/IZzhb

87. Thomas Friedman, "A Manifesto for the Fast World," *New York Times*, 28 March 1999, archive.today/aQHvy

instead to adorn the hidden fist like a velvet glove. Writing in 2013, Schmidt and Cohen stated,

What Lockheed Martin was to the twentieth century, technology and cyber-security companies will be to the twenty-first.[88]

---

88. Eric Schmidt and Jared Cohen, *The New Digital Age*, British paperback edition (John Murray, 2013), p. 98.

Google is committing to this ambition. Since the beginning of 2013, Google has bought nine experimental robotics and artificial intelligence companies and put them to work toward an undeclared goal under Andy Rubin, the former head of Google's Android division. See John Markoff, "Google Puts Money on Robots, Using the Man Behind Android," *New York Times*, 4 December 2013, archive.today/Izr7B

See also Adam Clark Estes, "Meet Google's Robot Army. It's Growing," *Gizmodo*, 27 January 2014, archive.today/mN2GF

Two of Google's acquisitions are leading competitors in the DARPA Robotics Challenge, a competition held by the Defense Advanced Research Projects Agency, with lavish Pentagon funding support for competitors. Schaft Inc, a Japanese company, is tipped to triumph at the DARPA competition with its entry—a bipedal, human-like robot that can climb stairs, open doors, traverse rubble, and is impervious to radiation. The other company, Boston Dynamics, specializes in producing running, walking, and crawling military robots for the Department of Defense. The most well known of Boston Dynamics' robots is "BigDog"—a horse-sized troop support carrier, which must be seen (on YouTube: is.gd/xOYFdY) to be believed. See Breezy Smoak, "Google's Schaft robot wins DARPA rescue challenge," *Electronic Products*, 23 December 2013, archive.today/M7L6a

See also John Markoff, "Google Adds to Its Menagerie of Robots," *New York Times*, 14 December 2013, archive.today/cqBX4

Google's real power as a drone company is its unrivaled collection of navigational data. This includes all the information associated with Google Maps and the locations of around a billion people. Once gathered, it should not be assumed that this data will always be used for benign purposes. The mapping data gathered by the Google Street View project, which sent cars rolling down streets all over the world, may one

One way of looking at it is that it's just business. For an American internet services monopoly to ensure global market dominance it cannot simply keep doing what it is doing, and let politics take care of itself. American strategic and economic hegemony becomes a vital pillar of its market dominance. What's a megacorp to do? If it wants to straddle the world, it must become part of the original "don't be evil" empire.

But part of the resilient image of Google as "more than just a company" comes from the perception that it does not act like a big, bad corporation. Its penchant for luring people into its services trap with gigabytes of "free storage" produces the perception that Google is giving it away for free, acting directly contrary to the corporate profit motive. Google is perceived as an essentially philanthropic enterprise—a magical engine presided over by otherworldly visionaries—for creating a utopian future.[89] The company has at times appeared anxious to cultivate this image, pouring funding into "corporate responsibility" initiatives

---

day be instrumental for navigating military or police robots down those same streets.

89. A utopianism occasionally bordering on megalomania. Google CEO Larry Page, for example, has publicly conjured the image of Jurassic Park–like Google microstates where Google is exempt from national laws and can pursue progress unimpeded. "The laws . . . can't be right if it's 50 years old; that's before the internet. . . . Maybe we could set apart a piece of the world. . . . An environment where people can try new things. I think as technologists we should have some safe places where we can try out new things and figure out the effect on society—what's the effect on people?—without having to deploy it to the whole world." See Sean Gallagher, "Larry Page wants you to stop worrying and let him fix the world," *Ars Technica*, 20 May 2013, archive.today/kHYcB

to produce "social change"—exemplified by Google Ideas. But as Google Ideas shows, the company's "philanthropic" efforts, too, bring it uncomfortably close to the imperial side of US influence. If Blackwater/Xe Services/Academi was running a program like Google Ideas, it would draw intense critical scrutiny.[90] But somehow Google gets a free pass.

Whether it is being just a company or "more than just a company," Google's geopolitical aspirations are firmly enmeshed within the foreign-policy agenda of the world's largest superpower. As Google's search and internet service monopoly grows, and as it enlarges its industrial surveillance cone to cover the majority of the world's population, rapidly dominating the mobile phone market and racing to extend internet access in the global south, Google is steadily *becoming* the internet for many people.[91] Its influence on the choices and behavior of the totality

---

90. The notorious mercenary security company Blackwater, best known for killing Iraqi civilians, was renamed Xe Services in 2009 and then Academi in 2011. See Jeremy Scahill, *Blackwater: The Rise of the World's Most Powerful Mercenary Army* (Nation Books, 2007).

91. Historically Google's success was built on the commercial surveillance of civilians through "services": web search, email, social networking, et cetera. But Google's development in recent years has seen it expand its surveillance enterprise by controlling mobile phones and tablets. The success of Google's mobile operating system, Android, launched in 2008, has given Google an 80 percent share of the smartphone market. Google claims that over a billion Android devices have registered themselves, at a rate now of more than a million new devices a day. See "Q1 2014 Smartphone OS Results: Android Dominates High Growth Developing Markets," *ABIresearch*, 6 May 2014, archive.today/cTeRY

See also "Android, the world's most popular mobile platform," on the Android Developers website: archive.today/5y8oe

of individual human beings translates to real power to influence the course of history.

If the future of the internet is to be Google, that should be of serious concern to people all over the world—in Latin America, East and Southeast Asia, the Indian subcontinent, the Middle East, sub-Saharan Africa, the former Soviet Union, and

---

Through Android, Google controls devices people carry on their daily routine and use to connect to the internet. Each device feeds back usage statistics, location, and other data to Google. This gives the company unprecedented power to surveil and influence the activities of its user base, both over the network and as they go about their lives. Other Google projects such as "Project Glass" and "Project Tango" aim to build on Android's ubiquity, extending Google's surveillance capabilities farther into the space around their users. See Jay Yarow, "This Chart Shows Google's Incredible Domination Of The World's Computing Platforms," *Business Insider*, 28 March 2014, archive.today/BTDJJ

See also Yasha Levine, "Surveillance Valley has put a billion bugs in a billion pockets," *Pando Daily*, 7 February 2014, archive.today/TA7sq

See also Jacob Kastrenakes, "Google announces Project Tango, a smartphone that can map the world around it," *Verge*, 20 February 2014, archive.today/XLLvc

See also Edward Champion, "Thirty-Five Arguments Against Google Glass," *Reluctant Habits*, 14 March 2013, archive.today/UUJ4n

Google is also aiming to become an internet access provider. Google's "Project Loon" aims to provide internet access to populations in the global south using wireless access points mounted on fleets of high-altitude balloons and aerial drones, having acquired the drone companies Titan Aerospace and Makani Power. Facebook, which bid against Google for Titan Aerospace, has similar aspirations, having acquired the UK-based aerial drone company Ascenta. See Adi Robertson, "Google X 'moonshots lab' buys flying wind turbine company Makani Power," *Verge*, 22 May 2013, archive.today/gsnio

See also the Project Loon website: archive.today/4ok7L

See also Sean Hollister, "Google nabs drone company Facebook allegedly wanted to buy," *Verge*, 14 April 2014, archive.today/hc0kr

even in Europe—for whom the internet embodies the promise of an alternative to US cultural, economic, and strategic hegemony.[92]

A "don't be evil" empire is still an empire.

* * *

By the time "The Empire of the Mind" eventually became *The New Digital Age: Reshaping the Future of People, Nations and Business*, published in April 2013, I had formally sought and received political asylum from the government of Ecuador, and taken refuge in its embassy in London. At that point I had already spent nearly a year in the embassy under police surveillance, blocked from safe passage out of the UK.[93] Online I noticed the press hum excitedly about Schmidt and Cohen's book, giddily ignoring the explicit digital imperialism of the title and the conspicuous string of pre-publication endorsements from famous warmongers like Tony Blair, Henry Kissinger, Bill Hayden and Madeleine Albright on the back.[94] I assumed it must

---

92. For an example of European concern, see Mathias Döpfner, "Why we fear Google," *Frankfurter Allgemeine*, 17 April 2014, archive.today/LTL6l

93. The police surveillance is ongoing at the time of writing, at a cost to the UK Treasury equivalent to $10 million. See Martin Robinson, "Julian Assange has cost Britain £6m as policing bill to guard Ecuadorian embassy where WikiLeaks fugitive is hiding soars," *Mail Online*, 25 April 2014, archive.today/RwwyH

94. Madeleine Albright is known for her prosecution of sanctions against Iraq, the NATO bombing campaign against Yugoslavia in 1999, and the expansion of NATO to the borders of Russia. She said that the death of 500,000 Iraqi children as a result of the sanctions regime was "worth it." See "Madeleine Albright says 500,000 dead Iraqi

be because it was powerfully argued. I had someone carry a copy past the police cordon so I could read it.

I was astonished. Billed as a visionary forecast of global technological change, the book failed to deliver—failed even to imagine a future, good or bad, substantially different to the present. The book was a simplistic fusion of Fukuyama "end of history" ideology—out of vogue since the 1990s—and faster mobile phones. It was padded out with DC shibboleths, State Department orthodoxies, and fawning grabs from Henry Kissinger. The scholarship was poor—even degenerate. It did not seem to fit the profile of Schmidt, that sharp, quiet man in my living room. But reading on I began to see that the book was not a serious attempt at future history. It was a love song from Google to official Washington. Google, a burgeoning digital superstate, was offering to be Washington's geopolitical visionary.

I waited for the stringent criticism the book would receive. But none came.[95] From the mainstream press and the tech sector there

---

Children was 'worth it'…wins Presidential Medal of Freedom from Obama" (video), uploaded 2 May 2012, youtu.be/omnskeu-puE

95. By the time my review had been published, the technology critic Evgeny Morozov—one of the very few writers with anything interesting to say on the intersection between technology and politics—had published his own critique of *The New Digital Age* in the *New Republic*. The article is well worth reading, as is his acerbic criticism of Apple's "purist" aesthetic, his scathing critique of the culture surrounding the TED conference circuit, and his dissection of the Silicon Valley jargon that is invading political language (the "2.0-ification of public discourse"). Morozov's writing has shaped my perspective on some of these issues.

On *The New Digital Age* see Evgeny Morozov, "Future Shlock," *New Republic*, 27 May 2013, archive.today/k3N7O

On Apple see Evgeny Morozov, "Form and Fortune," *New Republic*, 22 February 2012, archive.today/P2Vog

was only uncomprehending praise. Growing impatient, I reviewed it myself. The piece was published in the *New York Times* on June 2, 2013. I wrote that "as it encountered the big, bad world," Google had "thrown its lot in with traditional Washington power elements, from the State Department to the National Security Agency." Google apologists tried to dismiss the review as paranoid. But four days later, newspapers around the world were filled with the stories of Edward Snowden's NSA leaks. Front and center was the PRISM exposé, revealing the extent of what Eric Schmidt had been hiding when I had asked him, in June 2011, to leak the US government's data requests to WikiLeaks.

Some of the statements attributed to me in *The New Digital Age* did not sound like things I would have said. I had our archive department dig up the old recording, and I listened back. Sure enough, perhaps unsurprisingly given the level of the book's analysis, Schmidt and Cohen had misrepresented my words. As I listened to the recording I came to see the wider value of the discussion, and how the surrounding and subsequent events had given it a historical resonance.

The discussion contains strong and previously uncommunicated descriptions of the philosophy behind WikiLeaks and how technology affects power dynamics and social structures. It includes concepts for how to use decentralized technology to protect revolutionary activity—ideas I would love to see taken and implemented.

On TED see Evgeny Morozov, "The Naked and the TED," *New Republic*, 2 August 2012, archive.today/yTy2Q

On Silicon Valley jargon see Evgeny Morozov, "The Meme Hustler," *Baffler*, issue 22, 2013, archive.today/fQhqW

And at the level of symbolism, the discussion sees two different futures of the internet in conversation with each other: the one, a pervasive internet of centralized corporate governance; and the other, a vibrant, decentralized internet, fit for the emancipation of human history and human beings.

When Google Met WikiLeaks is the transcript of the discussion in book form. To make it more accessible for a general reader, OR Books and I have gone through the text and provided explanatory footnotes. Besides the transcript, I am including some other pieces of writing that lend it context. "The Banality of 'Don't Be Evil'" is my *New York Times* review of Schmidt and Cohen's book, now fully referenced. "Deliver Us from 'Don't Be Evil'" is a short overview of how WikiLeaks and the content of our discussion were represented (or misrepresented) in *The New Digital Age*. Throughout the book, references are made to various attempts by the US government and its allies to retaliate against WikiLeaks and its associates. Readers unfamiliar with these attempts can find a short summary, "Background on US v. WikiLeaks," at the end of the book. An accompanying website—when.google.met.wikileaks.org—contains a collection of raw extracts of leaked US State Department cables and Stratfor internal emails, released by WikiLeaks, along with other material that informs the critique made in these pages.

—Julian Assange
May 2014

THE BANALITY OF "DON'T BE EVIL"

This review of The New Digital Age *was originally published in the* New York Times *on June 2, 2013, shortly before the first documents from Edward Snowden were published in the* Guardian *and the* Washington Post.[96]

The New Digital Age is a startlingly clear and provocative blueprint for technocratic imperialism, from two of its leading witch doctors, Eric Schmidt and Jared Cohen, who construct a new idiom for United States global power in the twenty-first century. This idiom reflects the ever closer union between the State Department and Silicon Valley, as personified by Mr. Schmidt, the executive chairman of Google, and Mr. Cohen, a former advisor to Condoleezza Rice and Hillary Clinton who is now director of Google Ideas.

The authors met in occupied Baghdad in 2009, when the book was conceived. Strolling among the ruins, the two became excited that consumer technology was transforming a society flattened by United States military occupation. They decided the tech industry could be a powerful agent of American foreign policy.[97]

---

96. Julian Assange, "The Banality of 'Don't Be Evil,'" *New York Times*, 2 June 2013, archive.today/kxMZM

97. Eric Schmidt and Jared Cohen, *The New Digital Age*, British paperback edition (John Murray, 2013), pp. 8–11.

The book proselytizes the role of technology in reshaping the world's people and nations into likenesses of the world's dominant superpower, whether they want to be reshaped or not. The prose is terse, the argument confident, and the wisdom—banal. But this isn't a book designed to be read. It is a major declaration designed to foster alliances.

The New Digital Age is, beyond anything else, an attempt by Google to position itself as America's geopolitical visionary—the one company that can answer the question "Where should America go?" It is not surprising that a respectable cast of the world's most famous warmongers has been trotted out to give its stamp of approval to this enticement to Western soft power. The acknowledgments give pride of place to Henry Kissinger, who along with Tony Blair and the former CIA director Michael Hayden provided advance praise for the book.[98]

In *The New Digital Age* Mr. Schmidt and Mr. Cohen happily take up the white geek's burden. A liberal sprinkling of convenient, hypothetical dark-skinned worthies appear: Congolese fisherwomen, graphic designers in Botswana, anticorruption activists in San Salvador, and illiterate Masai cattle herders in the Serengeti are all obediently summoned to demonstrate the progressive properties of Google phones jacked into the informational supply chain of the Western empire.

The authors offer an expertly banalized version of tomorrow's world: the gadgetry of decades hence is predicted to be much like what we have right now—only cooler. "Progress" is driven by the inexorable spread of American consumer technology over the surface of the earth.

---

98. These endorsements are available on the Council on Foreign Relations website, where *The New Digital Age* has its own page, archive.today/rQtyh

Already, every day, another million or so Google-run mobile devices are activated.[99] Google will interpose itself, and hence the United States government, between the communications of every human being not in China (naughty China). Commodities just become more marvelous; young, urban professionals sleep, work, and shop with greater ease and comfort; democracy is insidiously subverted by technologies of surveillance and control; and our present world order of systematized domination, intimidation, and oppression continues, unmentioned, unafflicted, or only faintly perturbed.

The authors are sour about the Egyptian triumph of 2011. They dismiss the Egyptian youth witheringly, claiming that "the mix of activism and arrogance in young people is universal."[100] Digitally inspired mobs mean revolutions will be "easier to start" but "harder to finish."[101] Because of the absence of strong leaders, the result, or so Mr. Kissinger tells the authors, will be coalition governments that descend into autocracies.[102] They say there will be "no more springs" (but China is on the ropes).[103]

The authors fantasize about the future of "well resourced" revolutionary groups. A new "crop of consultants" will "use data to build and fine-tune a political figure."[104]

---

99. Donald Melanson, "Eric Schmidt: Google now at 1.5 million Android activations per day," *Engadget*, 16 April 2013, archive.today/wJh4i

100. Eric Schmidt and Jared Cohen, *The New Digital Age*, British paperback edition (John Murray, 2013), p. 122.

101. Ibid., p. 122, p. 128.

102. Ibid., p. 149.

103. Ibid., p. 144.

104. Ibid., p. 133.

"His" speeches (the future isn't all that different) and writing will be fed "through complex feature-extraction and trend-analysis software suites" while "mapping his brain function," and other "sophisticated diagnostics" will be used to "assess the weak parts of his political repertoire."[105]

The book mirrors State Department institutional taboos and obsessions. It avoids meaningful criticism of Israel and Saudi Arabia. It pretends, quite extraordinarily, that the Latin American sovereignty movement, which has liberated so many from United States–backed plutocracies and dictatorships over the last thirty years, never happened. Referring instead to the region's "aging leaders," the book can't see Latin America for Cuba.[106] And, of course, the book frets theatrically over Washington's favorite boogeymen: North Korea and Iran.[107]

Google, which started out as an expression of independent Californian graduate student culture—a decent, humane, and playful culture—has, as it encountered the big, bad world, thrown its lot in with traditional Washington power elements, from the State Department to the National Security Agency.

Despite accounting for an infinitesimal fraction of violent deaths globally, terrorism is a favorite brand in United States policy circles. This is a fetish that must also be catered to, and so "The Future of Terrorism" gets a whole chapter.[108] The future of terrorism, we learn, is

---

105. Ibid., p. 133.

106. Ibid., p. 144.

107. Ibid., throughout—for example, p. 166, pp. 96–97, et cetera.

108. Ibid., p. 151.

"cyber terrorism."[109] A session of indulgent scaremongering follows, including a breathless disaster-movie scenario, where cyber terrorists take control of American air-traffic control systems and send planes crashing into buildings, shutting down power grids and launching nuclear weapons.[110] The authors then tar activists who engage in digital sit-ins with the same brush.[111]

I have a very different perspective. The advance of information technology epitomized by Google heralds the death of privacy for most people and shifts the world toward authoritarianism. This is the principal thesis in my book *Cypherpunks*.[112] But while Mr. Schmidt and Mr. Cohen tell us that the death of privacy will aid governments in "repressive autocracies" in "targeting their citizens," they also say governments in "open" democracies will see it as "a gift" enabling them to "better respond to citizen and customer concerns."[113] In reality, the erosion of individual privacy in the West and the attendant centralization of power make abuses inevitable, moving the "good" societies closer to the "bad" ones.

The section on "repressive autocracies" describes, disapprovingly, various repressive surveillance measures: legislation to insert back doors into software to enable spying on citizens, monitoring of social

---

109. Ibid., p. 152, p. 162.

110. Ibid., p. 155.

111. Ibid., p. 162.

112. Julian Assange with Jacob Appelbaum, Andy Müller-Maguhn, and Jérémie Zimmermann, *Cypherpunks: Freedom and the Future of the Internet* (OR Books, 2012).

113. Eric Schmidt and Jared Cohen, *The New Digital Age*, British paperback edition (John Murray, 2013), pp. 57–64.

networks, and the collection of intelligence on entire populations.[114] All of these are already in widespread use in the United States. In fact, some of those measures—like the push to require every social-network profile to be linked to a real name—were spearheaded by Google itself.[115]

The writing is on the wall, but the authors cannot see it. They borrow from William Dobson the idea that the media, in an autocracy, "allows for an opposition press as long as regime opponents understand where the unspoken limits are."[116] But these trends are beginning to emerge in the United States. No one doubts the chilling effects of the investigations into the Associated Press and Fox's James Rosen.[117] But there has been little analysis of Google's role in complying with the Rosen subpoena.

---

114. Ibid., pp. 59–63.

115. Google's "Real Name Policy," which made it a terms of service violation to use a Google service under any name except a user's full legal name, was first introduced in 2011. Eric Schmidt personally endorsed the policy. See Matt Rosoff, "Google+ Isn't Just A Social Network, It's An 'Identity Service,'" *Business Insider*, 28 August 2011, archive.today/G5iRE

Google's policy immediately provoked what became known as the "Nymwars," a prolonged controversy among commentators, bloggers, and social network users on the importance of anonymity online. See Jillian York, "A Case for Pseudonyms," Electronic Frontier Foundation, 29 July 2011, archive.today/LhInw

See also Eva Galperin, "2011 in Review: Nymwars," Electronic Frontier Foundation, 26 December 2011, archive.today/bEYJd

116. These are Schmidt and Cohen's own words. Eric Schmidt and Jared Cohen, *The New Digital Age*, British paperback edition (John Murray, 2013), p. 75.

They are paraphrasing William Dobson, *The Dictator's Learning Curve: Inside the Global Battle for Democracy* (Doubleday, 2012).

117. In early May 2013 it emerged that the US Department of Justice, during an investigation into the source of a national security story, had secretly

I have personal experience of these trends.

The Department of Justice admitted in March 2013 that it was in its third year of a continuing criminal investigation of WikiLeaks. Court testimony states that its targets include "the founders, owners, or managers of WikiLeaks."[118] One alleged source, Bradley Manning, faces a twelve-week trial beginning tomorrow, with twenty-four prosecution witnesses expected to testify in secret.[119]

---

subpoenaed two months of the telephone records of twenty Associated Press reporters from the telecommunications company Verizon. The move was widely condemned as an attack on press freedoms. See Mark Sherman, "US government secretly obtained Associated Press phone records," Associated Press, 13 May 2013, archive.today/vyuNP

At around the same time the *Washington Post* reported that in the course of yet another criminal investigation by the Department of Justice into a journalistic source, the FBI had amassed a large store of surveillance data about the Fox News reporter James Rosen. Documents from the eventual espionage prosecution of the accused government source, Stephen Jin-Woo Kim, revealed that the Department of Justice had classified Rosen, a reporter, as an "unindicted co-conspirator" and labeled him a flight risk—implying that the basic practice of journalism is a criminal activity. See Ann E. Marimow, "A rare peek into a Justice Department leak probe," *Washington Post*, 20 May 2013, archive.today/LkTLR

See also "Justice Department affidavit labels Fox News journalist as possible 'co-conspirator,'" Fox News, 20 May 2013, archive.today/HBsA4

118. The reference to the "founders, owners, or managers" of WikiLeaks is from the court testimony of Special Agent Mark Mander from the US Army's Computer Crimes Investigation Unit, in the pre-trial hearings for the prosecution of Chelsea Manning.

119. This review originally went to press on the eve of Chelsea Manning's trial, after 1,103 days of pre-trial confinement. At the time, Chelsea Manning was known by the name Bradley. See Chelsea E. Manning, "Chelsea Manning announces gender transition—full statement," *Guardian*, 22 August 2013, archive.today/eMCdr

The New Digital Age is a balefully seminal work in which neither author has the language to see, much less to express, the titanic centralizing evil they are constructing. "What Lockheed Martin was to the twentieth century," they tell us, "technology and cyber-security companies will be to the twenty-first."[120]

Without even understanding how, they have updated and seamlessly implemented George Orwell's prophecy. If you want a vision of the future, imagine Washington-backed Google Glasses strapped onto vacant human faces—forever. Zealots of the cult of consumer technology will find little to inspire them here, not that they ever seem to need it. But this is essential reading for anyone caught up in the struggle for the future, in view of one simple imperative: know your enemy.

Chelsea Manning has since been convicted and sentenced to thirty-five years in prison. For more on the persecution of Chelsea Manning, see "Background on US v. WikiLeaks," page 205.

120. Eric Schmidt and Jared Cohen, *The New Digital Age*, British paperback edition (John Murray, 2013), p. 98.

ELLINGHAM HALL, JUNE 23, 2011

JA   Julian Assange   Editor in chief and founder of WikiLeaks.

ES   Eric Schmidt   Executive chairman of Google; coauthor of *The New Digital Age*; member of President Obama's Council of Advisors on Science and Technology; member of the Council on Foreign Relations.[121]

JC   Jared Cohen   Director of Google Ideas; coauthor of *The New Digital Age*; previously a member of the State Department's Policy Planning Staff and an advisor to Condoleezza Rice and Hillary Clinton; member of the Director's Advisory Board at the National Counterterrorism Center; adjunct senior fellow at the Council on Foreign Relations; cofounder of Movements.org.[122]

---

121. "About the author" in Eric Schmidt and Jared Cohen, *The New Digital Age*, British paperback edition (John Murray, 2013).

122. Ibid.

LS   Lisa Shields   Vice president, Global Communications and Media Relations for the Council on Foreign Relations; previously a TV producer for *Good Morning America* and *Primetime Live*.[123]

SM   Scott Malcomson   Communications director, International Crisis Group; editor of *The New Digital Age*; director of speechwriting for Ambassador Susan Rice at the US State Department in 2011–2012; life member of the Council on Foreign Relations.[124]

---

123. Shields's Council on Foreign Relations staff profile is available from www.foreignaffairs.com, archive.today/YSNrj

124. Malcomson's International Crisis Group staff profile is available from www.crisisgroup.org, archive.today/ETYXp

The following conversation was recorded at the house of Vaughan Smith in Norfolk, England, where I lived in 2011 under house arrest. A tracking beacon was attached to my ankle as a condition of my provisional release from jail. Three beacon relay antennas were installed in the house to report my movements to the British government.

The meeting began in the kitchen over lunch, continued briefly in a drawing room, and ended with a walk that was concluded by an approaching storm.

Some of my contributions have been lightly edited for brevity and ease of reading, but nothing of substance has been altered. I could not edit the words of the others without their involvement (I would not want to misrepresent them, after all). A very small number of minor changes to the order of the conversation have been made to improve its flow.

The full three-hour audio recording of the exchange can be listened to on the WikiLeaks website to demonstrate the integrity of the transcript.[125]

---

125. The audio recording has been published at:
www.wikileaks.org/Transcript-Meeting-Assange-Schmidt.html

FROM THOSE WHO SEE, TO THOSE WHO ACT

[*Beginning of tape*]

Eric Schmidt: Well, do you want us to start eating?

Julian Assange: Well, we can do both.

ES: Yeah, is that okay?

JA: So this is June 23. This is a recording between Julian Assange, Eric Schmidt, and . . .

Lisa Shields: Lisa Shields.

JA: Lisa Shields. To be used in a book by Eric Schmidt, due to be published by Knopf in October 2012.[126] I have been given a guarantee that I will see the transcript and will be able to adjust it for accuracy and clarity.[127]

ES: We agree.

---

126. The book was eventually published in April 2013 as *The New Digital Age: Reshaping the Future of People, Nations and Business.*

127. *The New Digital Age* was ultimately published without the promised consultation. The transcript here was produced by my team.

LS: We agree.

ES: Can we start? I want to talk a little about Thor. Right. The sort of, the whole Navy network . . .

JA: Tor or Thor?

ES: Yeah, actually I mean Tor.[128]

JA: And Odin as well.[129]

ES: All right, all right. Tor, and the Navy network. And I don't actually understand how all of that worked. And the reason I'm mentioning this is I'm fundamentally interested in what happens with that technology as it evolves. And so the problem I would assert is that if you're trying to receive data you need to have a guarantee of anonymity to the sender, you need to have a secure channel to the recipient, the recipient needs to be replicated. . . . What I'd like you to do if you could is talk a bit about that architecture, what you did in WikiLeaks technically, with the technical innovations that were needed and maybe also what happens.[130] How does it evolve? Technology always evolves.

JA: Let me first frame this. I looked at something that I had seen going on with the world, which is that I thought there were too many unjust acts. And I wanted there to be more just acts, and fewer unjust

---

128. Tor is free software designed to enable users to browse the internet anonymously. Early work on Tor was sponsored by the US Naval Research Laboratory. See the Tor Project website at www.torproject.org/about/overview

129. Odin, like Thor, was a Norse god.

130. For information about WikiLeaks see its website at wikileaks.org

acts. And one can ask, "What are your philosophical axioms for this?" And I say, "I do not need to consider them. This is simply my temperament. And it is an axiom because it is that way." That avoids getting into further unhelpful philosophical discussion about why I want to do something. It is enough that I do.

In considering how unjust acts are caused, and what tends to promote them, and what promotes just acts, I saw that human beings are basically invariant. That is, their inclinations and biological temperament haven't changed much over thousands of years. Therefore the only playing field left is: what do they have and what do they know? What they have—that is, what resources they have at their disposal, how much energy they can harness, what food supplies they have and so on—is something that is fairly hard to influence. But what they know can be affected in a nonlinear way because when one person conveys information to another they can convey it on to another, and another, in a way that is nonlinear.[131] So you can affect a lot of people with a small amount of information. Therefore, you can change the behavior of many people with a small amount of information. The question then arises as to what kinds of information will produce behavior which is just and disincentivize behavior which is unjust?

---

131. What is meant by "nonlinear" here is that the rate at which information spreads is not a constant, but instead increases as it spreads throughout a population. For example, if on one day a person spreads an idea to two people, and on the next day the three of them each spread it to two new people, and so on, then after the first day three people know, after the second day nine people know, after the first week 2,187 people know, and after twenty-one days every person on earth knows (given the present human population of 7.1 billion). In literal terms, "nonlinear" means "cannot be graphed as a straight line."

All around the world there are people observing different parts of what is happening to them locally. And there are other people that are receiving information that they haven't observed firsthand. In the middle there are people who are involved in moving information from the observers to the people who will act on information. These are three separate problems that are all tied together.

I felt that there was a difficulty in taking observations and, in an efficient way, putting them into a distribution system which could then get this information to people who would act upon it. You can argue that companies like Google, for example, are involved in this "middle" business of moving information from people who have it to people who want it. The problem I saw was that this first step was crippled, and often the last step was as well, when it came to information that governments were inclined to censor.

We can look at this whole process as justice produced by the Fourth Estate.[132] This description, which is partly derived from my experiences in quantum mechanics, looks at the flow of particular types of information which will effect some change in the end. The bottleneck appeared to me to be primarily in the acquisition of information that would go on to produce changes that were just. In a Fourth Estate context, the people who acquire information are sources; the people who work on information and distribute it are journalists and publishers; and the people who may act on it includes everyone. That's a high-level construct, but it then comes down to how you practically engineer a system that solves that problem, and

---

132. The "Fourth Estate" is an informal term referring to any group outside governmental or political organizations that have an influence on politics. It is usually used to denote the press.

not just a technical system but a total system. WikiLeaks was, and is, an attempt—although still very young—at a total system.

On the technical front, our first prototype was engineered for a very adverse situation where publishing would be extremely difficult and our only effective defense would be anonymity, where sourcing would be difficult (as it still currently is for the national security sector), and where internally we had a very small and completely trusted team.

ES: So here publishing means the question of the site itself, and making the material public?

JA: Yes, making the primary source material public. That's what I mean by publishing.

ES: So the first step was to make that done correctly?

JA: It was clear to me that all over the world publishing is a problem. Whether that is through self-censorship or overt censorship.

ES: Sorry, is that because of fear of retribution by the governments? Or all kinds of stuff?

JA: It's mostly self-censorship. In fact I would say that probably the most significant form of censorship, historically, has been economic censorship, where it is simply not profitable to publish something because there is no market for it. I describe censorship as a pyramid. On the top of the pyramid there are the murders of journalists and publishers. On the next level there are legal attacks on journalists and publishers. A legal attack is simply a delayed use of coercive force, which doesn't necessarily result in murder but may result in incarceration or asset seizure.

Remember the volume of the pyramid increases significantly as you go down from the peak, and in this example that means that the number of acts of censorship also increases as one goes down.

There are very few people who are murdered, there are a few public legal attacks on individuals and corporations, and then at the next level down there is a tremendous amount of self-censorship. This self-censorship occurs in part because people don't want to move up into the upper parts of the pyramid—they don't want to come under legal attack and coercive force, they don't want to be killed. That discourages people from behaving in a certain way. Then there are other forms of self-censorship motivated by concerns over missing out on business deals, missing out on promotions. Those are even more significant because they are lower down the pyramid. At the very bottom—which is the largest volume—is all those people who cannot read, do not have access to print, do not have access to fast communications, or where there is no profitable industry in providing such.[133]

We decided to deal with the top two sections of this censorship pyramid: threats of violence, and the delayed threats of violence that are represented by the legal system. In some ways that is the hardest case; in some ways it is the easiest case. It is the easiest case because it is clear-cut when things are being censored or not. It is also the easiest

---

133. For a visual representation of the censorship pyramid, see Marienna Pope-Weidemann, "Cypherpunks: Freedom and the Future of the Internet" (review), *Counterfire*, 13 September 2013, archive.today/Oyczc

For further discussion of this idea, see Julian Assange with Jacob Appelbaum, Andy Müller-Maguhn, and Jérémie Zimmermann, *Cypherpunks: Freedom and the Future of the Internet* (OR Books, 2012), pp. 123–124.

case because the volume of censorship is relatively small, even if the per-event significance can be very high.

Initially WikiLeaks didn't have that many friends. Although of course I had some previous political connections of my own from other activities, we didn't have significant political allies and we didn't have a worldwide audience that was looking to see how we were doing. So we took the position that we would need to have a publishing system where the only defense was anonymity. It had no financial defense; it had no legal defense; and it had no political defense. Its defenses were purely technical.

That meant a system that was distributed at its front[134] with many domain names, and a fast ability to change those domain names,[135] a

---

134. "Distributed at its front" is a technical description. The "front" of a website is the part that is visible when you visit it with your browser. On most news websites, the front and the back of the website are at the same physical location. This means that it is easier to censor, because there is just one point of weakness. WikiLeaks was built to deal with censorship, so it used a different model, where the back ends of the site are hidden and secret, and where the front end of the website is copied across lots of different computers. This means that even if one of the computers that hosts the "front" of the website is attacked, there will be other copies, and the site will still be available to the public. Furthermore, the "back" of the website remains secret, and new "front" nodes can be created at will.

135. A "domain name" is a human-readable name for an internet site, like "wikileaks.org" or "whitehouse.gov." All devices connected to the internet are assigned numerical addresses, known as IP addresses. All internet sites on the web are hosted on computers, and can be accessed with an IP address. For example, "195.35.109.44" is an IP address for the WikiLeaks website (just one of many front nodes). IP addresses are difficult to remember. To solve this problem, the "domain name system" (DNS) was invented: the system for linking "domain names" to IP addresses.

Unlike IP addresses, which are automatically assigned whenever you connect a device to the network, you can own a domain name of your caching system,[136] and, at the back, tunneling through the Tor network to hidden servers.[137]

---

choice by registering it with a "domain name registrar" for a small fee. All domain names are entered into a global directory—like a telephone directory—that links each domain name to the real IP address of an actual website. When "wikileaks.org" is typed into a browser, the browser first does a "lookup"—it contacts a DNS server, which contains a copy of the global directory, and looks up the domain name "wikileaks.org" to find the corresponding IP. It then loads the website from that IP. When a domain name is successfully translated into an IP address, it is said to have "resolved."

A "DNS attack" is an attempt to cut off an internet site by interfering with the directory that links the domain name to the IP address, so that it will no longer resolve. But just as there are many different telephone directories, there are many different DNS servers. By being able to switch DNS servers quickly, it is possible to defend against the effects of a DNS attack, and ensure that the website is accessible.

136. "A caching system," in the abstract, is a fast system that holds no information to begin with but is connected to a slow system that does. When the cache is asked for information, it initially relays the request to the slow system, forwards the reply, and keeps a copy. When the cache is asked again, it quickly sends the copy it has previously made.

WikiLeaks uses many location-shielding and encryption technologies that can slow down the path to the "back end," where the content is generated. In this context, a caching system is designed to help speed up the overall system, to make it more usable, by speeding up any repeated requests, which the majority of requests are.

137. A "hidden server," in this context, is a server that is not accessible using the conventional internet. WikiLeaks was using custom software to hide some of its websites in a way that was inaccessible to most of the internet.

The "back end" of WikiLeaks—that is, the software that produces the WikiLeaks website—was hidden. From the hidden "back end" the content was pushed to the front nodes by "tunneling through the Tor network," that is, using the location-hiding and encrypted Tor network to push content to the servers where people could read it.

ES: If I could talk just a little bit about this. So you can switch DNS, your website names and so forth very quickly.[138] You use the tunneling to communicate among these replicas? Or is this for distribution?

JA: We had sacrificial front nodes[139] that were very quick to set up which we nonetheless placed in relatively hospitable jurisdictions like Sweden.[140] Those front nodes were fast because there were very few hops between

---

The concept is similar to that of the "Tor hidden service." See the Tor Project website: archive.today/tmQ5y

138. "DNS" stands for "domain name system." For a more thorough explanation, see footnote 135, pages 71–72, on "domain name."

139. A "sacrificial front node" is just a copy of the front part of the website (see footnote 134, page 71, on "distributed at its front"), which is expected to be targeted by entities that want to censor WikiLeaks. Front nodes are cheap to set up, and can be quickly copied from a hidden server. The attacker will spend time going after sacrificial front nodes, but once they manage to take a front node down, more will quickly appear in its place, making censorship expensive and ultimately futile.

140. In the mid-2000s, Sweden was seen as a haven for internet users, with high connectivity (close to 90 percent of households in Sweden are connected to the internet) and technology-friendly policies implemented by the Swedish government. Many internet services that were under threat of censorship chose Sweden as an electronic refuge. Unfortunately, as the profile of services moving to Sweden increased, conflict grew between this feature of Sweden and the country's geopolitical relationships, especially with the United States. This led to a series of crackdowns (for example, the Pirate Bay trial) following pressure from the White House, as documented in WikiLeaks cables, and the subsequent flight of these services. Sweden has a population of only nine million, is geographically isolated, and proximate to a resurgent Russia. Ultimately, it did not have the geopolitical heft to risk offending its primary military and intelligence ally, the United States. See Rick Falkvinge, "Cable Reveals Extent Of Lapdoggery From Swedish Govt On Copyright Monopoly," *Falkvinge & co. on Infopolicy*, 5 September 2011, archive.today/r9jb4

them and the people reading them.[141] That's an important lesson that I had learned from things that I had done before—that being a Sherman tank is not always an advantage because you are not maneuverable and you are slow. A lot of the protection for publishers is publishing quickly. If you get information out quickly, and it is well read, the incentive for people to go after you in relation to that specific piece of information is close to zero. There may be broader incentives for them to go after you to teach a lesson to other people who might defy their authority, or to teach a lesson to your organization about the defiance of their authority in the future.

ES: So, again, to construct the argument, you were concerned that governments or whatever would attack the front ends of this thing through either denial of service attacks[142] or blocking, basically filtering them out,[143] which is commonly done. So an important aspect of this was to always be available.

JA: Always be available in one way or another. That's a battle that we have mostly won, but not completely. Within a few weeks the Chinese government had added us to their ban list. But we had hundreds of domain names, of various sorts, that were registered with very, very large DNS

---

141. "Very few hops" means that there were not many communication relays between the front nodes and the reader.

142. A "denial of service attack" (or DoS) is an attempt to make a website inaccessible by sending so many requests for access that the site is unable to respond to them all. This is a way of censoring a website by targeting the source of the website and effectively taking it down.

143. "Filtering," or content-control, is when an internet service provider blocks access to a website. This is a way of censoring a website by sitting in the middle, between an internet user and a website, and selectively interfering with the traffic.

providers, so that if there was DNS IP-level filtering[144] it would whack out another 500,000 domains as well as ours and that would create a political backlash that would make them stop. However, DNS-based filtering still hits us in China because the most common names—the ones that are closest to "WikiLeaks," the name that people can communicate easily—they are all filtered by the Chinese government.

ES: Of course they are.

JA: Any domain with "WikiLeaks" anywhere in it, no matter where it is, is filtered. So that means there has to be a variant that they haven't yet discovered. But the variant has to be widely enough known for people to go there. So there is a catch-22.

ES: That's a structural problem with the naming of the internet, but the Chinese would simply do content filtering on you.[145]

JA: Well, HTTPS worked for about a year and a half.[146]

---

144. "DNS-IP level filtering," in this context, means that the Chinese censorship system would actually block the IP addresses of the DNS servers that resolved the name "wikileaks.org" to the IP addresses for the WikiLeaks website. WikiLeaks countered this by registering with very large DNS servers that also had as many as half a million other domains on them. By IP-blocking these DNS servers, the Chinese censors would cause massive collateral damage, censoring hundreds of thousands of other websites along with WikiLeaks. The potential political backlash from such a move likely deterred the censors from taking this action.

145. "Content filtering" means blocking a website based on the content of the website, as opposed to simply blocking access to a particular domain name or IP address—so, for example, blocking any websites that mention WikiLeaks.

146. "HTTPS" stands for "Hypertext Transfer Protocol Secure," a protocol that encrypts connections between a browser and a server, or, in this case, between the browser of a person in China and the WikiLeaks web

ES: Okay.

[*Background noise, Jared Cohen and Scott Malcomson entering*]

JA: It worked quite well, actually. And then changing IPs also worked.[147] The Chinese internet filtering system is quite baroque. They have evolved it. Sometimes they do things manually and sometimes they do it in an automated way—adding IPs to the list based upon domain names. We had quite an interesting battle where we saw that they were looking up our IPs, and we saw that these requests came from a certain IP address block in China.[148] Whenever we saw that we just returned different IPs.[149]

---

server. HTTPS prevented the Chinese government from examining the data being transferred between the browser and the server, and therefore prevented the government from engaging in content filtering. However, ways of attacking this protocol have since been developed.

147. "Changing IPs" means changing the IP addresses. The Chinese censorship system worked by keeping a list of IP addresses that were to be blocked. By quickly switching to new IP addresses, the WikiLeaks site could be viewed by Chinese users, at least until the censors caught up and blocked the new IP addresses.

148. An IP block is a range of consecutive IP addresses, normally assigned as a package to an organization or a government department that plans on connecting many devices to the internet, and will have need of a large number of IP addresses. In this case, periodically computers within China were trying to look up the IP addresses for the domain name "wikileaks.org" The fact that all of these computers were within the same IP block showed that a single organization within China was performing regular lookups on "wikileaks.org" This was the first clue that it was the Chinese censorship system. This was confirmed after further investigation.

149. In order to block WikiLeaks in China, the Chinese censorship system had to use the domain name system to look up the IP addresses for WikiLeaks

ES: Ha-ha-ha-ha-ha. That's clever. Ha-ha-ha-ha-ha.

JA: I thought, we'll just return the Ministry of Public Security's IPs![150]

ES: That's funny. This is Jared Cohen, by the way.

Jared Cohen: Hi, I'm so sorry we're late. Flight delay.

JA: Pleased to meet you.

ES: Was it United or was it?

JC: Uh, Delta. Never flying again!

ES: Yeah, that's Delta.

JA: Larry?

JC: Jared.

JA: Jared! Jared.

ES: And this is Scott.

Scott Malcomson: Nice to meet you!

---

servers, which it could then block. But it was asking for WikiLeaks IP addresses on so regular a basis that it was possible to distinguish the censors from normal traffic. It was then possible to selectively feed the censors false information about which web servers were controlled by WikiLeaks, causing them to block bogus servers, and not the real ones. Regular visitors to the WikiLeaks site from China were unaffected.

150. Causing the Ministry of Public Security, which runs the Chinese censorship system, to add *itself* to the list of internet sites to be censored.

ES: Scott is our editor.

SM: Sorry, we're an hour and a half late.

JA: That's all right! It's a beautiful day to drive!

ES: We've actually been having a perfectly wonderful time.

SM: I'm sure. I'm sure. I'm sure.

LS: Julian was kind enough because we did not bring a tape recorder!

ES: Ha-ha-ha-ha-ha.

LS: Quite embarrassing, I must add, that you ask to interview some-one and you have to borrow a tape recorder.

JA: A friend of mine did an interview in Fiji during General Rabuka's coup, where he had General Rabuka's second in command admit, on tape, that the CIA had paid him off.[151]

ES: Wow.

JA: And he got back. And he was like, yes! This is the story of the decade! And the tape had failed. I have lots of these now. You should always have multiples!

[*Laughter*]

ES: Always, always have your own.

---

151. General Sitiveni Ligamamada Rabuka led two coups in Fiji in 1987 to overthrow the ethnic Indian–dominated government that had been voted into power, to replace it with one composed of indigenous Fijians.

ES: For Scott and Jared's benefit, we spent a fair amount of time just sort of chatting about Google, and what I was up to. I introduced Lisa. I failed to properly articulate what a brilliant book we're working on. And Lisa assisted me. Julian seemed to be okay with her assist. What we agreed was that we would talk about technology directions and maybe the implications of all of this. And the deal was that this would be on the record for the book. We would have a transcript prepared, which he would have an opportunity to modify, extend, and improve its clarity, which all seemed incredibly reasonable to me.

We just started. We talked a little bit about the general principles that he's articulated, and I was just starting to talk a little bit about the structure—why WikiLeaks has been architected the way it is. And the rough summary there is that the concern that he had in architecting this was that, if you look at the governments you know the stuff that they do—murder journalists, imprison journalists, and that kind of stuff. His view was that you want to attack that problem by making a system that was very, very hard to block. So the nontechnical explanation of what he did is that he built a system where if they do the obvious things to block them it can simply show up in another way. Change its name and have replicas.

THE NAMING OF THINGS

JA: The naming of things is very important. The naming of human intellectual work and our entire intellectual record is possibly the most important thing to be done. We all have words for different objects, like "tomato." We use a simple word, "tomato," instead of actually describing every little aspect of this goddamn tomato.[152] Because it takes too long to describe this tomato precisely, we use an abstraction so that we can think and talk about it. And we do that also when we use URLs.[153] Those are frequently used as a short name for some human intellectual content. We build all of our civilization, other than on bricks, on human intellectual content. We currently have a system with URLs where the structure we are building our civilization on is the worst kind of melting Plasticine imaginable. That's a big problem.

ES: And you would argue a different namespace structure should evolve that more properly allows—

---

152. Objects on the table were used throughout the conversation to demonstrate concepts via their spatial relationships.

153. "URL" stands for "uniform resource locator," another name for a human-readable web address, like https://www.wikileaks.org/donate

JA: I think there is a fundamental confusion, an overloading of the current URL idea.

ES: Yep. Absolutely.

JA: On the one hand you have live dynamic services and organizations that run those services—meaning a hierarchy, a system of control, be it an organization, a government, or some controlling group. And on the other hand you have human intellectual artifacts that can be completely independent from any system of human control. They are out there in the Platonic realm.[154] They should be referred to in a way that is intrinsic to their intellectual content, and not in a way that is dependent on an organization. I think that is an inevitable and very important way forward.

I first saw that this was a problem when dealing with a man by the name of Nadhmi Auchi.[155] A few years ago he was listed by one of the big business magazines as the fifth richest man in the UK. An Iraqi, he worked for the Iraq Oil Ministry and grew rich before leaving for Britain in the early 1980s. He is alleged by the Italian press to have been involved in a lot of arms trading. He has over a hundred companies run out of his Luxembourg holding unit and several that we discovered under his wife's name in Panama. He infiltrated the British Labour political establishment to the degree

---

154. The "Platonic realm," in this context, means the universe of possible knowledge. The phrase has its origins in Plato's theory of forms, but the most enjoyable exploration is the famous short story "The Library of Babel" by Argentinian author Jorge Luis Borges (1899–1986), available online at archive.today/Fm4fM

155. See the WikiLeaks page on Nadhmi Auchi at archive.today/BkT0D

that on his business's twentieth birthday celebration in London he was given a painting signed by 130 ministers and members of Parliament, including the then prime minister Tony Blair.

Nadhmi Auchi was a financier of Tony Rezko, who in turn was a fundraiser for Rod Blagojevich from Chicago, the former governor of Illinois. Both Rezko and Blagojevich have now been convicted of corruption. Tony Rezko was also an intermediary who helped Barack Obama buy part of his residential home.

This is detail but it will get to a point. During the 2008 presidential primaries a lot of attention was turned to Barack Obama by the US press, unsurprisingly. They started to look into his fundraisers and discovered Tony Rezko, and then they started to turn their eyes toward Nadhmi Auchi. Auchi then hired Carter-Ruck, a rather notorious firm of London libel solicitors, whose founder, Peter Carter-Ruck, has been described as doing for freedom of speech what the Boston Strangler did for door-to-door salesmen.[156] He started writing letters to all the London newspapers that had records of his 2003 extradition to France and conviction for fraud in the Elf Aquitaine scandal, in which he had been involved in channeling illegal commissions on the sale of Kuwaiti-owned oil refineries while Kuwait was under Iraqi occupation before the first Gulf War.[157]

---

156. The Boston Strangler was a serial killer active in Boston, Massachusetts, during the early 1960s. He is said to have posed as a door-to-door salesman in order to trick women into letting him into their apartments.

157. The story would come full circle when the French investigating magistrate involved, Eva Joly, would go on to investigate corrupt Icelandic banks, run for president in the 2012 French presidential elections, lose, be elected to the European Parliament, and then come to the embassy in which I reside to try and find a solution to my four years of detention without charge in the United Kingdom.

So the *Guardian* pulled six articles from 2003 without saying anything. They had been in the *Guardian*'s archive for five years. If you go to those URLs you will not see "removed due to legal threats," you will see "page not found." There is also an article from the *Telegraph* and a bunch from some American publications and bloggers, and so on. Important bits of recent history that were relevant to an ongoing presidential campaign in the United States were pulled out of the intellectual record.[158] They were also pulled out of the *Guardian*'s index of articles. So although the *Guardian* is published in print and you can go to the library and look up those articles, how would you know that they are there to look up, because they are not there in the *Guardian*'s index? Not only have they ceased to exist, they have ceased to have ever existed. It is the modern implementation of Orwell's dictum: "Who controls the past controls the future; who controls the present controls the past"—because all records of the past are stored physically in the present.[159]

This issue of preserving politically salient intellectual content while it is under attack is central to what WikiLeaks does, because that's what we are after. We're after those bits[160] that people are trying to suppress because we suspect, usually rightly, that they're expending economic work on suppressing those bits because they perceive that those bits are going to induce some change.

---

158. WikiLeaks has restored them to the historical record. See archive.today/oOCks

159. George Orwell, *Nineteen Eighty-Four* (Secker and Warburg, 1949).

160. "Bits" here is used in the sense of information theory—i.e., "those bits," "that information."

SM: So it's the evidence of the suppression that you look for in order to determine value?

JA: Yes . . . not precisely but that's a very good—

SM: Well, tell me precisely.

JA: Well, it's not always right. But it's very suggestive—

SM: It's not perfect!

JA: It's not perfect but it is a very suggestive signal that the people who know the information best—i.e., the people who wrote it—are expending economic work in preventing it going into the historical record, preventing it getting to the public. Why spend so much work doing that? It's more efficient to just let everyone have it—you don't have to spend time guarding it, but also you are more efficient in terms of your organization because of all the positive unintended consequences of the information going around. So we selectively go after that information, and that information is selectively suppressed inside organizations, and very frequently, if it is a powerful group, as soon as someone tries to publish it, we see attempts at post-publication suppression.

ES: I want to know a little more about the technology. So in this structure, you basically can put up a new front very quickly and you have stored replicas that are distributed. One of the questions I have is how do you decide which ISPs?[161]

---

161. "ISP" stands for "internet service provider." In this context an ISP is a company that provides communications links or server space with which to run an internet site. When choosing an ISP for a publisher like WikiLeaks it is necessary to consider some hard questions, such as, "Will

JA: That's a very good question.

ES: Yeah, it is a pretty complicated set of questions.

JA: I will give you an example of how not to choose them. We dealt with a case in the Turks and Caicos Islands where there was a great little group called the *TCI Journal* (*Turks and Caicos Islands Journal*).[162] They are a bunch of political reformers, ecologically minded people who live there and saw that overseas property developers were coming in and somehow getting Crown land very cheaply and building big high-rises on it and so on.[163] They were campaigning for good governance and trying to expose these people.

It's a classic best-use case for the internet: cheap publication means that we can have many more types of publishers, including self-subsidizing publishers. People are able to publish purely for ideological reasons or for altruistic reasons, because the costs of altruism in relation to publishing are not so high that you can't do it.

They were hounded out of the Turks and Caicos Islands pretty quickly. They moved their servers to India. The property developer that they had been busy exposing then hired correspondent lawyers in London, who hired correspondent lawyers in India who hounded them out of their ISP there. They moved to Malaysia; they got hounded out, same deal—they became

this ISP stand by you against censorship attempts, or will it censor you itself?"

162. The Turks and Caicos Islands are a British Overseas Territory in the Caribbean.

163. As the Turks and Caicos Islands are a British Overseas Territory, the Crown—the British monarchy—formally owns public land.

unprofitable to the ISP as soon as the legal letters started arriving. They went to the US and their US ISP didn't fold—they picked one that was a bit better. The editors were anonymous because of the threats, although the columnists often weren't, but the responsible party, in the publishing sense, was anonymous. However, it was noticed that they were using a Gmail address, and so the property developers filed suit in California and as part of that they started issuing subpoenas, including on Gmail. The result was that Google told the *TCI Journal* that they had to come to California to defend themselves, otherwise everything would be handed over.

These are little guys in the Turks and Caicos Islands trying to stop corruption in their country against a property developer with vast resources. How can they go to California to fight off a subpoena which is part of a bogus libel suit? Well, of course they can't. But we managed to arrange some lawyers for them, and there just happened to be a great bit of the California statute code that addressed this precise situation, which is when someone publishes something and then you issue a subpoena to try and get their identity. You can't do it and you have to pay costs. That was a nice little legal hook that someone had introduced. Google didn't send any lawyers to help them.

That's an example of what happens if you're pretty bright guys—they had a good Indian technical guy, they had bright political guys—and you come together to try and fix corruption in your country using the internet as your publishing mechanism. What happens? You are hounded from one end of the earth to the other! These guys were lucky in that they had enough resources to survive this hounding, and they ended up finding some friends and settling into a position where they are all right.

For us this was a matter of looking at which ISPs had survived pressure. Because I have been involved in politics, technology, and anti-censorship for a long time I knew some of the players. We had ISPs that we had already infiltrated ideologically, where we had friends. We knew that they would fight in our corner if a request came in, and we knew there was a decent chance that if subpoenas were served, even with a gag order, we'd soon find out about it.

Could someone do this who is not in that world? Not easily. You can look at ISPs that WikiLeaks is currently using, or that the Pirate Bay has used, or other groups that are tremendously under attack.[164] It is often a little ISP that is like this. There's a little ISP called PRQ in Sweden that was founded by Gottfrid, whose pseudonym is anakata—he's one of the technical brains

---

164. The Pirate Bay was started in 2003 by my friend Gottfrid Svartholm (nickname "anakata"), who also worked for WikiLeaks as a consultant. He was subsequently prosecuted by Sweden after pressure from the United States (documented in WikiLeaks cables), later rendered from Cambodia by the Swedish intelligence service SAPO, tried again in Sweden, and then extradited to Denmark, where he is currently facing trial. The Pirate Bay is a BitTorrent tracker, which enables sharing of large files between computers connected on the internet by coordinating communication between them. Its website, blocked in many locations, is www.thepiratebay.se See Kristina Svartholm, "Gottfrid Svartholm Warg: a year of his life from his mother's perspective," WikiLeaks, 18 August 2013, is.gd/h2MeG4

See also Rick Falkvinge, "Cable Reveals Extent Of Lapdoggery From Swedish Govt On Copyright Monopoly," *Falkvinge & co. on Infopolicy*, 5 September 2011, archive.today/r9jb4

behind the Pirate Bay.[165] They had developed a niche industry, along with Bahnhof, a bigger ISP in Sweden, dealing with refugee publishers—and that is the correct phrase for it; they are publishing refugees.[166]

PRQ had, other than WikiLeaks, the American Homeowners Association, which had to flee from property developers in the United States; the Kavkaz Center, a Caucasus news center which is constantly under attack by the Russians (in fact PRQ was raided several times by the Swedish government after leverage from the Russian government); the Rick A. Ross Institute for the Study of Destructive Cults, an American outfit which had been sued out of America by Scientology.[167]

Another example is *Malaysia Today*, run by a wonderful guy by the name of Raja Petra who has two arrest warrants out for him

---

165. In addition to his association with the Pirate Bay and PRQ, Gottfrid Svartholm has been a WikiLeaks consultant who collaborated on the Collateral Murder video release (on which see footnote 237, page 141; the video is available at youtu.be/5rXPrfnU3G0). Most of those who feature on the Collateral Murder video credits have subsequently been harassed. Gottfrid himself has been through protracted legal battles. For more information and documents about his legal case see "Prosecution and prison documents for Pirate-Bay founder Gottfrid Svartholm Warg (alias Anakata)," WikiLeaks, 19 May 2013, archive.today/aOsLB

166. For more information on PRQ see its website at www.prq.se
    For more information on Bahnhof see its website at www.bahnhof.net

167. The Kavkaz Center reports from Chechnya with an Islamic perspective. For more information see archive.today/djebS
    The Rick A. Ross Institute for the Study of Destructive Cults, Controversial Groups, and Movements is now known as the Cult Education Institute. For more information see archive.today/8PQ4K

in Malaysia. He has fled to London, but his servers can't survive in London; they are in Singapore and the United States.[168]

ES: But again [*indistinct*] there are a lot of other sites that participate in this.

JA: Yes, we have some fourteen hundred; we have mirrors that are voluntary.[169]

ES: So those are basically opt-in mirror sites?

JA: They determine their own risks. We don't know anything about them. We can't guarantee that they are at all trustworthy, but they do increase the numbers.

ES: You have been quoted in the press as saying that there is a much larger store of information that is encrypted and distributed. Is it distributed in those sorts of places?

JA: No, we openly distribute encrypted backups of materials that we view as highly sensitive, that we are to publish in the coming year.[170]

ES: Got it.

---

168. *Malaysia Today* is a popular Malaysian news blog. In 2008 the Malaysian government temporarily blocked it, and the site's founder, Raja Petra Kamarudin, was imprisoned for months. For more information see archive.today/6S0QZ

169. A "mirror" is an exact replica of a website.

170. An "encrypted backup" is a copy of the material that is kept separately in case something happens to the original. The copy is encrypted using a secret key or password so that only those with access to the key can decrypt it and read it.

JA: Not, as some people have said, so that we have a "thermonuclear device" to use on our opponents, but rather so that there is very little possibility that that material will be taken from the historical record, even if we are completely wiped out.

ES: And eventually you will reveal the key that is necessary to decrypt it?

JA: No. Ideally, we will never reveal the key.

ES: I see.

JA: Because there are things like redactions that sometimes need to be done on this material.

ES: Sure.

JA: Our view is that the material is so significant that even if we released it as is, with no redactions, the benefits would outweigh the harm. But through redacting things we can get the harm down even more.

ES: And I understand that. One more technical question about the front end: my simple explanation is that the tools will get better for an anonymous sender to send to a distrustful recipient, and then this anonymous [*noise*] you're describing. It will get to the point where there will be a very large amount of people using such services for all sorts of reasons: truthful, lying, manipulation, what have you. The current technology you use, basically you had FTP bundles sent to you. Basically people will FTP up something and just sort of ship it to you.[171]

---

171. "FTP" stands for "file transfer protocol," one of the methods used to send files over the internet. It is not used by WikiLeaks, but used here by Schmidt to represent any method of sending files over the internet.

JA: No, we have lots of different paths, and that's quite deliberate, and we don't say which one is used more than which other one because that means that opponents' investigative resources have to be spread across all possible paths. That could mean in-person. Or in the mail—postal mail is still actually pretty good if you want to send anonymous stuff; encrypt something to a key if you think it might be intercepted on the way and send it. Or straight HTTPS uploads, although they are not actually direct, but to the user it looks like they are that way. Behind the scenes all sorts of other stuff is going on. The biggest problem with computer security is not communication, it's end points.

ES: Right.

JA: The biggest problem is dealing with end point attacks both on someone trying to send us information and more importantly on our end point that receives information.[172] If someone trying to send us information is compromised, that's one compromise of one person. If our end point that receives information is compromised, that's a potential compromise of every person that's trying to send us material.

ES: I guess I didn't ask my question quite right. Is there some new technology which in your view would materially change this simple model that I have about the vast increase of—

---

172. "End point attacks" (i.e., spyware implanted by an intelligence agency or computer virus) are attacks aimed at compromising one of the "end points"—in other words, either the computer sending the information or the computer receiving the information. When two computers are communicating using properly implemented, strong encryption, it becomes infeasible to sit in the middle, intercept, and read the content of their communication. The only way to read the content is to perform an end point attack.

JA: Yes.

ES: So what are those technologies?

JA: The most important one is naming things properly. If we are able to name a video file or a piece of text in a way that is intrinsically coupled to the information contained there, so that there is no ambiguity, then it permits this information to be spread in such a way that you don't have to trust the underlying networks.[173] And you can flood it.[174] A secure hash is an example of this, but there are variants—maybe you want a way that human beings can actually remember.[175]

---

173. This means that you do not have to worry whether the companies and telecommunications systems transferring or storing the information have modified it in some way.

174. A "flood network" distributes information by having each host send a copy of any new information to every host that it is connected to. In this manner it is similar to a river in flood pushing water down every connected tributary. Provided there are no isolated hosts, every host will receive the new information eventually, as every path is taken. Since every path between hosts is traversed, the fastest path is also traversed.

175. A "hash algorithm" or "hash function" is a formula that takes data of any size and turns it into a "hash": a number (represented by a sequence of characters of a standard length) that can be used to refer to the original data. An example of an insecure hash in everyday life is the use of acronyms to denote names that are too long to use in practice, for example "NATO" for the "North Atlantic Treaty Organization." In this case, the formula is a very simple one: "take the first letter of each word."

More typical "hash functions" are mathematical formulas for taking information of arbitrary length and crunching it into a unique hash of a short, fixed length. A secure hash uses a formula so complex that even though a modest computer can create a hash from an input, even the most powerful computer cannot go the other way—it cannot create an original input that would make a particular hash. For example, given NATO, it could not find either "North Atlantic Treaty Organization" or an alternative, such as "Never Again Trust

ES: Why don't you have to trust the underlying networks?

JA: Because you can sign the hashes.[176]

ES: You can sign the name as well as the content?

JA: You can just sign the hash.

ES: Right, sign the hash.

JA: If the name is like a hash.

ES: Then it's unambiguous as to what it's representing.

JA: It's unambiguous, yes.

ES: You're basically saying you have a provable name as opposed to an alterable name.

JA: Yes. And those sorts of mechanisms are evolving now. We have been using something like this internally. I've been writing a paper

---

Obama." Of course, "take the first letter of each word" is not a secure hash function, and it is therefore easy to move from the hash to an input that makes it, but this is not true of secure hash functions.

A secure hash is dozens of characters long, instead of the four used in the example here, making it hard for a human being to remember. For example, the SHA256 hash of the secret location of WikiLeaks' next mega leak is: 66d9563648f3f23b2c90065a831e9357f2721bd3965b95e1e88a7e510c76026a.

Try figuring that one out.

The broader philosophical difficulty being discussed is called "Zooko's Triangle."

176. In this context, "sign" means the author or publisher of the information uses a digital signature scheme to produce a publishable electronic "signature" that proves that the hash was created by them. See "Public-Key Cryptography," *Wikipedia*, archive.today/2ue3r

on it to try and make this a standard for everyone, but you can see it is actually evolving. If we look at magnet links, have you seen these? There is an enhancement of BitTorrent which is a magnet link. A magnet link is actually a hash, so it is hash addressing.[177] It doesn't point to any particular server; rather, there is a big distributed hash tree.[178] I don't know how technical I can get.

---

177. BitTorrent is a peer-to-peer file-sharing protocol: a way for internet users to share files with each other in a decentralized way. The further development of the BitTorrent protocol has been driven by the need for a distributed method of sharing files that does not rely on any one point of failure. The "magnet link" is an extension of the BitTorrent protocol to provide even greater resistance to censorship.

A magnet link is a secure hash (and some other information, which isn't important here) of a file. It is used as a "file name" by newer versions of the BitTorrent protocol to find copies of the requested file located on multiple, untrusted computers without going through a central directory. Hence there is no central point of attack that could be used to censor the distribution of particular files.

As such, magnet links are an evolutionary step toward the consistent naming of intellectual content.

178. A hash tree is a hierarchical structure composed of hashes of hashes.

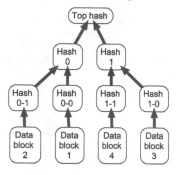

ES: Please.

JA: There is a big distributed hash tree over the many millions of computers involved and many entry points into this hash tree so it is very hard to censor. And the addressing for content is on the hash of the content.

ES: Right, so you are basically using the hash as the address, and you do the addressing within the namespace to provide it. So as long as you have a signed name you can't hide it.

JA: Well, there's a question as to what it tells you. You've got a name of something, you've got a hash, but what does that tell you? Nothing really, because it is not really readable by a human. So you need another mechanism to point out that something is important to you—for example, WikiLeaks signing something and saying that it is—

ES: An interesting piece of information.

JA: —an interesting piece of information, and we have verified that it is true.[179] Once you feed that information into the system then it becomes very unclear how it got into the system or how you could

---

In this picture of a hash tree, every unit above the data blocks contains the hash of the information of the units below it; so Hash 0-0 contains the hash of Data block 1, Hash 0 contains the hash of Hash 0-0, and Hash 0-1, and so on. See "Merkle Tree," *Wikipedia*, archive.today/zfXgV

With a "distributed hash tree," the hashes that make up the hash tree are distributed over multiple computers.

179. In other words, using a digital authentication scheme where WikiLeaks publishes a digital signature of the hash to say that this hash corresponds to a document WikiLeaks has authenticated and published—just like a publisher's imprint on the inside cover of a book, but impossible to fake.

get rid of it from the system. And if someone does manage to get rid of it, you know for sure that it has been got rid of, because the hash doesn't resolve to anything anymore. Similarly, if someone were to modify it, the hash changes.[180]

SM: I was just going to say, why wouldn't they just rename it?

JA: They can't because the name is intrinsically coupled to the intellectual content.

ES: I think the way to explain this, to summarize the technical idea is: take all the content of a document and come up with a number; so if the content is gone, the number doesn't show anything, and if the content has changed, the number doesn't compute right anymore. So it's distinguishing properly. So how far are we from this type of system being deployable?

JA: On the publishing end, the magnet links and so on are starting to come up. There's also a very nice little paper that I've seen in relation to Bitcoin.[181] Do you know about Bitcoin?

---

180. Using a naming system like the one proposed, where the name is a hash based on the content of the thing it names, if anything changes about the content, the hash also changes. For example, the SHA256 hash for "Putin rode a horse" is 1284ffaa16df7c406c4528045e491f86cc3c57a9661a203aa-97914c19a09a0df. But if the message is tampered with, the hash changes. The SHA256 hash for "Putin rogered a horse" is 9b24760c2ae1eba3cb8a-f2a8d75faadd5cd4dcb492fdb31ce60caafa3eb8597e.

  Similarly, if the content is erased entirely, the hash remains, a reminder that that content existed, and a sign that something has been suppressed.

181. Bitcoin is a type of digital currency based on encryption. Like any other form of money it can be exchanged for dollars or other currencies or used

ES: I do not.

JA: Okay, Bitcoin is something that evolved out of the cypherpunks a couple of years ago.[182] It's a stateless currency.

SM: Yeah, I was reading about it just yesterday.

JA: It is very important, actually. It has a few problems, but its innovations exceed its problems. Now, there have been innovations along these lines in many different paths of digital currencies— anonymous, untraceable, et cetera. People have been experimenting with them over the past twenty years. Bitcoin actually has the balance and incentives right, and that's why it is starting to take off. It has no central nodes; it is all point-to-point.[183] One does not need to trust any central mint.

---

to buy items, but there is no central bank and, unlike with fiat currencies, it is not controlled by state power.

The paper being referred to is actually an internet post on the Bitcoin Forum about the development of Namecoin, another, similar currency derived from the Bitcoin concept: archive.today/aY5j0

182. "Cypherpunks advocate for the use of cryptography and similar methods as ways to achieve societal and political change. Founded in the early 1990s, the movement has been most active during the 1990s 'cryptowars' and following the 2011 internet spring. The term cypherpunk, derived from (cryptographic) cipher and punk, was added to the *Oxford English Dictionary* in 2006." From Julian Assange with Jacob Appelbaum, Andy Müller-Maguhn, and Jérémie Zimmermann, *Cypherpunks: Freedom and the Future of the Internet* (OR Books, 2012).

183. No one single computer is the source of all Bitcoins, unlike most currencies, for which there is a single agency (a central mint) that is responsible for printing all the money. Instead, as the fundamental unit of a Bitcoin is based on finding special hashes, any computer with enough computing

If we look at traditional currencies such as gold, we can see that they have interesting properties that make them valuable as a medium of exchange. Gold is divisible, it is easy to chop up; in fact out of all metals it is the easiest to chop up into fine segments. You can tell relatively easily whether it's true or whether it's fake. You can take chopped-up segments and you can put them back together by melting the gold. That's what makes it a good medium of exchange. It's also a good store of value, because you can bury it in the ground and it's not going to decay, unlike apples or steaks.

The problem with previous digital currencies on the internet is that you have to trust the mint not to print too much of it. And the incentives for the mint to keep printing are pretty high, because you can print free money. That means you need some kind of regulation. And if you have regulation, who is going to enforce that regulation? All of a sudden you have sucked into this issue the whole problem of the state, with all of the political pressures as people try to get control of the mint to push it one way or another for their particular purposes.

Bitcoin instead has an algorithm where anyone can be their own mint. They're basically just searching for collisions with hashes.[184] They

---

power can "mine" or produce Bitcoins. For more information see the "Mining" section on the Bitcoin wiki: archive.today/LidYs

184. A hash collision is when two texts encode to the same hash. For example, if our hash function was "take the first letter of each word," then an example collision would be hash(North Atlantic Treaty Organization) = NATO = hash(Never Again Trust Obama). Collisions are impossible for a secure hash, by definition, but Bitcoin uses an algorithm known as HashCash in which the difficulty of the collision problem is fine-tuned so that it is increasingly hard over time, but not impossible.

are searching for a sequence of zero bits on the beginning of the thing, and they have to search randomly. So there is a lot of computational work required in order to do this. That work algorithmically increases as time goes by. So the difficulty in producing Bitcoins becomes harder and harder and harder. That is built into the system.

ES: Right, right. That's interesting.

JA: Just like the difficulty of mining gold becomes harder and harder and harder, and that's what makes people predict that there is not going to be a sudden amount of gold on the market.

ES: It enforces scarcity.

JA: Yes, it enforces scarcity. Scarcity will increase as time goes by. What does that mean for incentives for going into the Bitcoin system? It means that you should get into the Bitcoin system now.[185] You should be an early adopter because your Bitcoins are going to be worth a lot of money one day. A Bitcoin address is just a big hash of

---

Computers connected to the Bitcoin system crunch numbers all day looking for special hash collisions. When they find one, a Bitcoin is created. This computational work requires electricity, and hence Bitcoin's scarcity is derived from energy scarcity, providing an insurmountable physical limit on the speed at which Bitcoins can be created. Similarly the energy required to mine gold or silver creates scarcity for these metals, which prevents sudden inflation.

185. On the day of the conversation, Bitcoin had risen above the US dollar and reached price parity with the Euro. By early 2014 it had risen to over $1,000, before falling to $430 as other Bitcoin-derived competing crypto-currencies started to take off. WikiLeaks' strategic investments in the currency saw more than 8,000 percent return in three years, seeing us through the extralegal US banking blockade.

a public key that you generate.[186] Once you have this hash you can just advertise it to everyone, and people can send you Bitcoins. There are people that have set up exchanges to convert from Bitcoin to US dollars and so on.

The way Bitcoin has been designed solves a very interesting technical problem: how do you stop double spending with a digital currency? All digital material can be cloned at almost zero cost, so if you have currency as a digital string of numbers, how do you stop me copying it? I want to buy this piece of pasta; here is my digital currency.[187] But I have taken a copy of my digital currency. And now I want to buy your bit of egg with it. And now I want to buy your radish! And you say, "What? I've already got that piece of currency! What's going on here? There has been some fraud committed here!" There's a synchronization problem. Who now has the coin?[188]

---

186. The term "public key" is derived from public-key encryption, also known as asymmetric-key encryption, which is a kind of encryption system that uses a combination of two different keys: a private key and a public key. See "Public-Key Cryptography," *Wikipedia*, archive.today/WwkHK

    One example of public-key encryption that has been developed for email is the free, open-source encryption program Pretty Good Privacy (PGP), originally developed by Phil Zimmermann. For more information see the website of the OpenPGP Alliance: www.openpgp.org

187. A prop from the table is being used again.

188. In other words, if there are two copies of a Bitcoin, how do you know which is the real Bitcoin and which is the copy? The answer is in the design. Bitcoin is a peer-to-peer network, with no central authority. The economic history of Bitcoin—which Bitcoins belong to which accounts—is distributed to unrelated computers all around the world; hence the "synchronization problem"—all the computers must constantly update their information from each other to make sure that they have the same view about the economic history of the Bitcoin world. In this way a consensus is

There is a point-to-point spread network with all these problems of some parts of the network being faster, some parts of the network being slower, multiple paths of communication; how do you solve this synchronization issue to determine who has the coin? This is, to my mind, the real technical innovation of Bitcoin—it has solved it by using some hash problems which enforce delay trees and then a delay time. CPU work has to be done in order to move one thing to another, so information can't spread too fast.

Once we have a system of currency that is easy to use like that, then we can start to use it for other things that we want to be scarce. What things do we want to be scarce? Well, names. We want short domain names to be scarce; otherwise, if they are not scarce, if it doesn't take work to get them, as soon as you have a nice naming system some ass-hole is going to come along and register every short name for himself.[189]

ES: Right. That's very interesting.

JA: So this Bitcoin replacement for DNS is part of precisely what I wanted and what I was theorizing about, which is not a DNS system, but rather a short-bit-of-text to long-bit-of-text tuple registering service.[190] Because that is the abstraction. With domain

---

determined between all of the machines connected to the Bitcoin network as to which Bitcoin transactions are valid and which are counterfeit.

189. If you want to know why short domain names are valuable, imagine if your website address was www.thelongestdomainnameintheworldandthensomeandthensomemoreandmore.com, particularly if you do not know how to touch type.

190. A "tuple" here is just a name, value pair. For example, (name, phone number) or (domain name, IP address) or, in this case, (human memorizable name, secure hash).

names and all these problems you have something that you want to register that is short, and you want to couple that to something that is longer or unmemorable.

For example, take the First Amendment. The phrase "US First Amendment" is a very short phrase, but it expands to a longer bit of text.[191] So you take the hash of this longer bit of text, and now you have got something that is intrinsically coupled to it, but it's unmemorable. But then you can register "US First Amendment" coupled to the hash. That then means you have a structure where you can tell whether something has been published or unpublished. One piece of human intellectual information can cite another one in a way that can't be manipulated. If it is censored, the censorship can be found out. And if it is censored in one place you can scour the entire world for this hash, and no matter where you find it you know it is precisely what you wanted.

ES: Right.

JA: So that, in theory, permits human beings to build up an intellectual scaffold where every citation, every reference to some other part of human intellectual content, is precise, and it can be discovered if it exists out there anywhere at all, and it is not dependent on any particular organization. As a way of publishing, this seems to be the

---

191. The phrase "US First Amendment" (three words long) actually stands for the entire content of the United States First Amendment, which is: "Congress shall make no law respecting an establishment of religion, or prohibiting the free exercise thereof; or abridging the freedom of speech, or of the press; or the right of the people peaceably to assemble, and to petition the Government for a redress of grievances."

Its SHA256 hash is 69be9b199c542c56183c408a23d7fd41f-c878ec2634be6583db1659fb0e91063.

most censorship-resistant manner of publishing possible, because it is not dependent on any particular mechanism of publishing. You could be publishing through the post, you could be publishing on conventional websites, you could be publishing using BitTorrent or however, but the naming is consistent.

Publishing is also a means of transferring. If you want to transfer something anonymously to one particular person, all you have to do is encrypt the information with their key and publish it.

ES: Basically this entire system depends on revocable and irrevocable key structures. Are you worried that the key structures will fall apart?

JA: In terms of the naming part, the hashing, it doesn't depend on a key structure at all. In terms of the keys, Bitcoin has its own key structure, and that's an independent thing. There are all sorts of problems with that—hackers can come in and steal keys, et cetera. These are the same problems that you have with cash. Armored vans are needed to protect cash. There are some enhancements you can use to try and remove the incentives one way or another. For example, you could introduce a sub-currency with fixed periods of spends, so you could retract for one week or one day, and a merchant will accept it or not accept it.

ES: But the average person doesn't understand that when RSA was broken into, an awful lot of very important keys involving commerce were taken, presumably by the Chinese.[192]

---

192. In 2011, RSA Security, which sells encryption to government agencies, military contractors, and banks, was hacked, and a number of private keys were stolen. Subsequently, it has been reported that the stolen keys were used to break into companies—for example, Lockheed Martin.

JA: The public key structure is a tremendous problem, in the same way that domain name structures are a tremendous problem. The browser-based public key system that we have for authenticating what websites you are visiting is awful. It is truly awful. The number of people that have been licensed to mint keys is out of control. There are some that have gone bankrupt and been bought up cheaply by Russian companies. We can assume—I have been told by someone who is in the know, although I am not yet willing to put it on the public record because I only have one source, so just between you and me—that Verisign has actually given keys to the US government. Not all, but signed particular keys.[193]

That's a big problem with the way things are authenticated presently. There are some traditional alternative approaches, like PGP has a web of trust.[194] I don't think those things really work. What I think does work is something close to what SSH does.[195]

---

193. This is still unconfirmed at the time of writing, although subsequent court records reveal that secret orders for the subversion of encryption keys were issued against other US companies. See the Lavabit case: Megan Geuss, "Lavabit goes head-to-head with feds in contempt-of-court case," *Ars Technica*, 29 January 2014, archive.today/zLrEs

194. "Web of trust" is a decentralized trust model used with PGP (Pretty Good Privacy) that avoids having to rely on a central authority or hierarchy. It is a public model of the trust relationships between its users, which is impossible to fake because it is built on strong cryptography. But the cryptography also ensures that the trust relationships, once published, are comprehensively undeniable: they cannot be faked. If you are someone who really needs to use cryptography, you probably should not be putting work into cryptographically authenticating and publishing your trust relationships with "co-conspirators."

195. "SSH" stands for "secure shell." It is a protocol that is used to make an encrypted connection between computers. In particular, SSH can be used as a "remote shell," a program that lets you log in to another computer remotely and control it by sending it commands. The original remote shell

That's probably the way forward. It is opportunistic key registration. So as part of your interaction, the first time you interact, you register your key, and then if you have a few points of keying and some kind of flood network, then you can see that lots of people have seen that key many times in the past.[196]

ES: I think my summary would be that this notion of a hash idea of the name is a very interesting one, because I had not linked it to Bitcoin, or that kind of approach, with scarcity. That's a new idea for me. Have you published that idea?

JA: Not the link to Bitcoin. The paper that came out about coupling something to Bitcoin was just trying to address the DNS issue.[197]

---

programs, such as "RSH" or "telnet," used insecure connections, meaning that attackers could listen in to the connection, and subvert it; SSH, which was invented during the 1990s cryptowars by Finnish programmer Tatu Ylönen, uses encrypted connections, which prevent such attacks.

The first time SSH connects to a remote computer, it learns that computer's public key. Every time it connects after that, it checks the computer against the original key to make sure no attacker is modifying the connection. As long as the first connection is not intercepted, no subsequent connection can be either.

196. On traditional opportunistic keying systems like SSH, the initial connection is the most vulnerable. If an attacker feeds you a fake key on the initial connection, it can interfere with all of your subsequent connections without being detected.

The idea here is to use a "flood network" to share keys, automatically using the experiences of others to create a consensus about the true keys, so that even during the initial connection, an attacker will be easy to spot.

This idea can be seen in a variant for SSL called TACK (Trust Assertions for Certificate Keys) by Moxie Marlinspike. See www.tack.io

197. The paper being referred to is actually an internet post on the development of Namecoin: archive.today/aY5j0

But fortunately, the guy who did it understood—why limit it to IP addresses? It's natural to make the thing so that it could go to any sort of expansion.

The idea that there should be this naming system and the importance of preserving history and making these scaffolds and mapping out everything—that's on the site. I think it's part one of the Hans Ulrich Obrist interviews.[198]

ES: I think we should study this quite a bit more so we generally understand it. Maybe we'll have a few more questions about it. The other comment I would make is that, on the assumption that what you are describing is going to happen, which I think is probable, given that the incentive structure is—

JA: Oh, I've had these ideas several years but now I see other people are also getting into—

ES: Well, there are enough people who are interested in solving the problem you are trying to solve. On the internet you see a lot of [*inaudible*]. What I am thinking of is how would I attack it? How would I attack your idea? And I still think I would go after the signing and the key infrastructure. So if I can break the keys . . .

For more information on the ideas behind Namecoin, the Bitcoin Forum thread titled "BitDNS and Generalizing Bitcoin" is indispensable: archive.today/9kEmz

Also of interest is an excellent and prescient essay by Aaron Swartz on "Zooko's Triangle." Aaron Swartz, "Squaring the Triangle: Secure, Decentralized, Human-Readable Names," aaronsw.com, archive.today/pIvtj

198. "In Conversation with Julian Assange Part I," WikiLeaks, 23 May 2011, archive.today/E9IOb

JA: There are different parts of the idea. It's quite interesting as to when something has gone from being unpublished to published. If you spread some information and you've got it well labeled using a hash, that hash is important. It has to spread in another way, say, by WikiLeaks signing the hash. But there are many ways for it to spread. People could be swapping that hash in email. They could be telling each other on the telephone, et cetera.

ES: You are saying that all of these systems do not have a single point of attack. I can break down your HTTPS but you can still use the US Postal Service to send it, for example.

JA: Exactly, and you would know that you were getting the right thing because of its naming. It is completely accurate.

COMMUNICATING IN A REVOLUTIONARY MOMENT

ES: When we were chatting initially we talked about my idea that mobile phones being empowered is changing society. A rough summary of your answer, for everybody else, is that people are pretty much the same, and something big has to change their behavior; this might be one of them. You said you were very interested in somebody building phone-to-phone encryption. Can you talk a little bit about, roughly, the architecture where you would have a broad open network and you have person-to-person encryption? What does that mean technically, how would it work, why is it important? That kind of stuff. I think people don't understand any of this area, in my view.

JA: When we were dealing with Egypt we saw the Mubarak government cut off the internet, but there was one ISP still connected. Quite a few of us were involved in trying to keep it open. It had maybe 6 percent of the market.[199] The Mubarak government also cut off the mobile phone system. Why is it that this can be done? People with mobile phones have a device that can communicate in a radio spectrum. In a city there is a high density of mobile phones. There is

---

199. The ISP is Noor Group. It actually had about 8 percent of the market share.

always a path between one person and another person; that is, there is always a continuous path of mobile phones, each one of which can, in theory, hear the radio of the others.

ES: So you could form a peer-to-peer network.[200]

JA: In theory you could form a peer-to-peer network. Now, the way most GSM phones and other phones are being constructed is that they receive on a different frequency to that on which they transmit, and that means that they cannot form peer-to-peer networks.[201] They have to go through base stations.[202] But we are seeing now that mobile phones are becoming more flexible in terms of base station programming. They need to become more flexible because they are sold in different markets where different frequencies are used and there are different forms of wireless output.[203] Even when mobile phones are not sufficiently flexible, we are seeing that WiMAX might be coming along, which will give them

---

200. The basic idea is called a "mesh network." Each phone relays its communications through the other phones within range, instead of having to relay these communications through the antennas and networks of mobile phone companies.

201. "GSM" stands for "Global System for Mobile Communications" and is the primary telecommunications standard for mobile phones the world over. A GSM phone is just a regular cell or mobile phone.

202. The cell phone towers owned by the mobile phone companies.

203. For example, to achieve economies of scale, cell phone manufacturers have been moving to create phones that will work in most countries. This means the phone must be compatible with various frequencies and types of wireless encoding standards used in each country, much the way a universal power adaptor has adaptable pins for the variation in power sockets across different countries.

greater radius for two-way communications.[204] But also it is getting very cheap to make your own base station. There is software now that will run a base station for you.[205] So you can throw these things up and pretty quickly make your own networks using conventional mobile phones. In fact this is what is done to cheaply spy on mobile phones—you set up a fake base station. There are vans now that you can buy in bulk on the commercial spy market. You set up a van and intercept mobile phone calls.

During revolutionary periods the people involved in the revolution need to be able to communicate in order to plan quickly, and they need to be able to pass around information about what is happening in their environment so that they can dynamically adapt to it and produce the next strategy. If only the security services are able to communicate, and the government turns the mobile phone system off, the security services have a tremendous advantage.[206] If you have a system where individuals are able to communicate securely and robustly despite what the security services are doing, then the security services will have to give more ground. It's not that the government is necessarily going to be overthrown, but rather they have to make more concessions.

---

204. WiMAX is the Worldwide Interoperability for Microwave Access standard, a type of wireless data communication encoding standard that often works at greater distances than what is widely available now.

205. See OpenBTS: www.openbts.org

206. A recent example of this occurred in 2011 in San Francisco. In order to thwart #OpBART, a planned protest against a series of lethal shootings by the Bay Area Rapid Transit Police, the authorities shut down a number of cell phone base stations covering the San Francisco transport system.

ES: They have their networks. So your argument is that even with existing mobile phones, they could be modified to have peer-to-peer encrypted tunnels for voice and data, presumably.[207]

JA: Voice is a bit harder. I designed a prototype. It only works for medium-sized groups. It is a peer-to-peer UDP-encrypted flood network.[208] UDP permits you to put lots and lots of cover traffic in, because you can send random data to random internet hosts.[209]

ES: Oh, this is clever. So that way you can't be blocked, right?

JA: Yes.

ES: Because UDP is a single packet, right?

JA: Right, so you send it to random internet hosts, and a random internet host doesn't respond, which is exactly the same as a host that is receiving stuff. Using this you can do hole-punching through firewalls.[210] It means that normal at-home people can use this; they

---

207. A tunnel here is a channel of communication between two parties via third-party relays.

208. "UDP" stands for "User Datagram Protocol," a simple, fast internet protocol used for sending a single packet of information from one internet host to another.

209. That is, by picking random internet addresses.

210. Most internet users are behind a "firewall" or another mechanism (such as "Network Address Translation," otherwise known as NAT) that blocks the receipt of connections initiated by another party. When two such users wish to communicate with each other directly, they cannot. Hole-punching is a technique to trick firewalls or NATs into establishing direct

don't need to have a server.[211] And it is very light bandwidth, so you can put it on mobile phones as well.[212]

The killer application is not lots of voice.[213] Rather, it is chat rooms. Small chat rooms of thirty to a hundred people—that is what revolutionary movements need. They need it to be secure and robust. The system I made was protocol independent.[214] You've got your encapsulating thing—UDP or whatever—and in theory you could be pushing it over SMS, you could be pushing it over TCP, or however.[215] You could be using a mobile phone, you could be using a desktop computer, et cetera. You can put all of that into one big mesh, so that all you need, even when the whole country is shut off, is one satellite connection out, and your internal network connects to the rest of the world.

ES: Yeah, yeah.

---

communication, as opposed to having to relay communications through a third-party server, which may not be reliable or trusted.

211. In this context "server" means an internet-connected computer that can accept incoming connections.

212. It is light bandwidth because the data sent is minimal, being concisely composed from encrypted text encoded into a UDP packet.

213. A "killer application" (or killer app) is a computer program that is so useful or popular that in itself it makes whatever it is associated with worth having.

214. That is, not limited to UDP, meaning people using different types of connections would be able to communicate.

215. "TCP" or "Transmission Control Protocol" is the most common internet protocol. It is used, for instance, to communicate most website content. It is more complex than UDP.

JA: If it's a small network you can use flood. A flood network takes every possible path; therefore it must take the fastest possible path. A flood network will always find a way but it doesn't scale to large quantities. But if you've got a good routing system you just need one link out. And in Egypt we had people who hacked Toyota in Cairo, took over their satellite uplink, and used it to connect to this ISP that had 6 percent of the market. That sort of thing was going on all the time. There was a hacker war in Egypt to try and keep this more independent ISP up and running. But it shouldn't have been so hard. It should have been the case that all you need is just one connection, and then the most important information can get out.

Look how important Twitter and SMS are. Human beings are pretty good at encoding the most important thing that's happening into a short amount of data. There are not that many human beings. There just aren't that many.

ES: It's not a bandwidth problem.[216]

JA: It's not a bandwidth problem. All you need is one pipe and you can connect a country that is in a revolutionary moment to the rest of the world.[217] And just as important, you can connect points within that country, cities within that country. It's not that hard a thing to do, quite frankly.

---

216. That is, the problem is not one of limited electronic communications capacity.

217. "One pipe" here means that just a single international telecommunications link is needed for information to flow out of a country to the wider network.

ES: Scott, do you want to?

SM: It's hard to stop! It's so interesting!

ES: I actually have like five hours' more technical questions.

SM: I know! Because it's like one thing, and then there's more.

ES: How would you architect this, how would you architect that . . . ?[218]

---

218. "Architect" is tech-talk for "design."

CENSORSHIP IS ALWAYS CAUSE FOR CELEBRATION

SM: I am just wondering, on the human side of this—you have such experience of the world that you described earlier. I had three hours' sleep, so forgive me if I don't remember exactly what you said, but the combination of technical and altruistic people, and what amounts to a kind of subculture that you've been involved in for some fifteen years now. So you know how that subculture works. And that subculture needs to either stay the same or expand in order to do the work that you are describing. And so, since our book is about ten years away—

JA: It has dramatically expanded.

SM: What are the patterns there in terms of the people part rather than the technical part?

JA: That's the most optimistic thing that is happening—the radicalization of internet-educated youth. People who are receiving their values from the internet and then, as they find them to be compatible, echoing them back. The echo back is now so strong that it drowns the original statements completely.

The people that I've dealt with from the 1960s' radicals who helped liberate Greece and fight Salazar in Portugal, they say that this moment in time is the most similar there has been to what happened in that period of liberation movements.[219]

SM: Do you see it scaling differently than it did in the sixties?

JA: I wasn't alive in the 1960s, but as far as I can tell, in the West— because there are certain regions of the world I am unaware of— their statement is true. The political education of apolitical technical people is extraordinary. Young people are going from apolitical to political. It is a very, very interesting transition to see.

SM: This is your world. Why do you think that took place?

JA: Fast communication; critical mass of young people; newer generation; and then some catalyzing events. The attack on WikiLeaks was a catalyzing event, and our success in defending against this attack was a catalyzing event. Do you remember the PGP case, the grand jury with Zimmermann?[220]

---

219. Authoritarian conservative António de Oliveira Salazar was the prime minister and de facto dictator of Portugal from 1932 until 1968. His Estado Novo government survived him until 1974, when it was overthrown by a leftist military coup, and democracy was restored.

After a coup d'état in 1967, Greece was ruled by a US-backed military junta known as the "Regime of the Colonels," which was overthrown by a democratic uprising, also in 1974.

This was a significant time for southern Europe. The Spanish dictator, Francisco Franco, died just a year later, in 1975, handing over power to King Juan Carlos I, who facilitated the restoration of Spanish democracy.

The period is covered in depth by WikiLeaks' Kissinger Cables. See www.wikileaks.org/plusd

220. In 1991, when Phil Zimmermann released PGP, cryptography programs were classified as munitions under US federal law and could not be exported. Because PGP was on the internet, and someone outside the

ES: He had a lot of fun with that.

JA: I wrote half a book on that. It was never published, because my co-writer went and had children.

[*LS spills water all over her note-taking laptop. JA quickly grabs her laptop and turns it upside down.*]

LS: Oh no, ha-ha-ha-ha!

ES: Ha-ha-ha!

JC: Why do I feel that has happened before?

LS: That was really funny.

SM: So much for the historical record!

JA: As I said, multiple copies!

[*Laughter*]

ES: Why don't you save whatever you were doing?

SM: Get it into the name tree before everything goes wrong.

US had downloaded the program, Zimmermann was considered to have exported his program. Consequently, he was under investigation for three years by a US federal grand jury. During the 1990s the NSA and FBI were behind a campaign to stop the spread of cryptography that became known as the "cryptowars" (for more on the cryptowars, see footnote 236, page 135). After the statute of limitations had expired, Zimmermann subsequently admitted to having intentionally uploaded PGP to the internet as an attempt to spread cryptography before it could be banned.

LS: Did you see how fast he was? It was like an impulse.

JC: Yeah, I almost feel like you were there before the computer even got water on it.

ES: Computers are important in our line of work.

[*Laughter*]

LS: That was sweet, thank you. Go right ahead.

SM: But young people aren't inherently good. And I say that as a father and with regret.

[*Laughter*]

JA: Oh no, I think that actually . . . Well, I've read *Lord of the Flies* and I went to thirty different schools, so I've seen plenty of *Lord of the Flies* situations.[221] But no, I think that the instincts human beings have are actually much better than the societies that we have.

ES: Than the governments, basically.

JA: I am not going to say governments. The whole structure of society. The economic structure. People learn that simple altruistic acts don't pay off, and they see that some people who act in nonaltruistic ways end up getting Porsches, and it tends to pull them in that direction. I thought about this a while ago when I saw this fantastic video

---

221. *Lord of the Flies* is a novel by William Golding about a group of school-boys marooned on a desert island, revealing the darker side of human nature as societal restraints break down. William Golding, *Lord of the Flies* (Faber and Faber, 1954).

that came out of Stanford in 1971 on nuclear synthesis of DNA.[222] Have you seen it?

SM: No.

JA: It's on YouTube. It's a wonderful thing. It's explaining nuclear synthesis through interpretive dance. There are, like, 130 Stanford students out there in the middle of a sports field pretending to be DNA: a whole bunch pretending to be a ribosomal subunit, all wearing the hippy clothes of the day. But they were actually all very bright people. It was a very good bit of education; it is not that it was cool and unusual—rather it was extremely instructive, and before computer animation it was the best representation of how a ribosomal unit behaves. Could you see Stanford doing that now? Absolutely impossible. Stanford is far too conservative to do that now, even though it was extremely effective. You can bet that everyone who was in that dance remembers exactly how nuclear synthesis occurs, because they all had to remember their parts. And I remember it having seen it.

The period of peak earnings for the average wage in the United States was, what, 1977?[223] Then certain things happened. Those people who were altruistic and not too concerned about

---

222. "Protein synthesis: an epic on the cellular level," Stanford University Department of Chemistry, 1971. Available on YouTube at youtu.be/u9dhO0iCLww

223. Depending on how you crunch the numbers, the peak male median income was at some point in the mid- to late 1970s. See page 50 of Carmen DeNavas-Walt, Bernadette D. Proctor, and Jessica C. Smith, "Income, Poverty, and Health Insurance Coverage in the United States: 2012," US Department of Commerce, Economics and Statistics Administration, US Census Bureau, September 2013, is.gd/xJ9wPV

finances and fiscalization simply lost power relative to those people who were more concerned about finances and fiscalization, who worked their way up in the system. Certain behaviors were disincentivized and others were potentiated. That is primarily, I believe, as a result of the technology that enables fiscalization. So, fast bank transfers, the IRS being able to account for lots of people—it sucks people into a very rigid fiscalized structure.[224]

You can have a lot of political "change" in the United States, but will it really change that much? Will it change the amount of money in someone's bank account? Will it change contracts? Will it void contracts that already exist? And contracts on contracts? And contracts on contracts on contracts? Not really. So I say that free speech in many Western places is free not as a result of liberal circumstances but rather as a result of such intense fiscalization that it doesn't matter what you say. The dominant elite doesn't have to be scared of what people think, because a change in political view is not going to change whether they own their company or not; it is not going to change whether they own a piece of land or not. But China is still a political society, although it is rapidly heading toward a fiscalized society. And other societies, like Egypt, are still heavily politicized. Their rulers really do need to be concerned about what people think, so they expend proportionate efforts on controlling freedom of speech.

See also Katie Sanders, "Time's Rana Foroohar says median male worker hasn't seen a raise in 30 years," *PolitiFact*, 15 January 2014, archive.today/u6q5b

224. "IRS" is the Internal Revenue Service, the US government agency responsible for tax collection.

But I think young people actually innately have fairly good values. Of course it's a spectrum, but they have fairly good values most of the time and they want to demonstrate them to other people, and you can see this when people first go to university. They become hardened as a result of certain things having a payoff and other things not having a payoff.

SM: But let me tease out some of this. It sounds like you've got a view of the globe with certain societies where the impact of technology is relatively slight, certain societies where politically the impact of technology could be quite great, and certain societies where it would be a sort of middling way. And you would put China into, I guess, the middling category. Since our book is all about technology and social transformation ten years down the line, what's the globe that you see given the structure you are describing?

JA: I am not sure about the impact on China. It is still a political society, so the impact could be very great. I often say that censorship is always cause for celebration. It is always an opportunity because it reveals fear of reform. It means that the power position is so weak that you have got to care what people think.

JC: That's an interesting argument.

ES: This is a very interesting argument.

SM: It's like you find the sensitive documents by watching them hunt.

JA: Exactly. So when the Chinese expend all this energy on censoring in novel ways, do we say that it is a complete waste of time and energy, or do they have a whole bunch of experience managing the country and understand that it matters what people think? I say it's much more reasonable to interpret it as meaning that the different actors within China who are able to control that censorship system understand correctly that their power position is weak and they need to be careful what people think. So they have to censor.

SM: So the state is rational, at least in its repression.

JA: I'm always worried when talking about the state because it's all individuals acting in their own perceived interest. This group or that group.

SM: Fair enough.

JA: Take the people who work as censors at the Ministry of Public Security in China. Why do they censor, and what do they censor first? I'll tell you what they censor first—they censor the thing that someone in the Politburo might see! That's what they censor first. They are not actually concerned about darknets.[225]

JC: Sorry, about?

JA: They are not concerned about darknets because their bosses can't see what is on the darknet, and so they can't be blamed for not censoring it.

---

225. A group of computers connected over the internet where each computer only knows the addresses of a few others participating in the larger darknet network. A darknet is difficult for a government to censor, but on the other hand a darknet is also comparatively difficult to access. I2P is an example of a darknet: www.i2p2.de

We had this fantastic case here in the UK where we published a whole bunch of classified documents from the UK military. Then later on we did a preemptive FOI, which we do occasionally on various governments where we can.[226] We did it on the UK Ministry of Defense to see whether they were doing some investigation in response, so we could better protect our sources. At first they did not give us the documents. We appealed, and got back a bunch. They showed that someone in the MoD had spotted that there was a whole lot of UK military documents on our website about their surveillance program, and another two-thousand-page leak from them about how to stop things leaking, which stated that the number one threat to the UK military was investigative journalists.[227] So that had gone to some counterintelligence person, and they had said, "Oh my god, there are hundreds of pages, and it is about all sorts of countries and it just keeps going, it's endless, it's endless!!!!!" Five exclamation marks. That was the discovery phase; now the "what is to be done" phase. BT has the contracts for the MoD.[228] They told BT to censor us from them. So everyone in the UK MoD could no longer read what was on WikiLeaks. Problem solved!

---

226. "FOI" stands for "freedom of information" request, a request for information that is legally available from a public body in countries with a Freedom of Information law.

227. "UK Ministry of Defence continually monitors WikiLeaks: eight reports into classified UK leaks, 29 Sep 2009," WikiLeaks, 30 September 2009, archive.today/6pMbw

228. BT, formerly British Telecom, is the largest telecommunications company in the UK and one of the largest in the world.

ES: Interesting.

JA: Their generals and their bosses could no longer see that we had MoD stuff on WikiLeaks. Now there are no more complaints, and their problem is solved. Understandings like this might be quite advantageous to use in some of these systems. If you understand that bureaucratic structures always have this sort of thing going on, that means darknets are going to have a pretty easy time of it, until they are so big that they are not darknets anymore.

SM: That's really, really interesting. You mentioned investigative journalism. You've had a lot of experience with journalism by now, in many different respects. How do you see the kind of freeing of information that you were describing earlier, as fitting into journalistic processes, if at all? Or is it replacing it?

JA: No, it is more how these journalistic processes fit into something that is much bigger. The much bigger thing is that we as human beings shepherd and create our intellectual history as a civilization. And it is that intellectual history on the shelf that we can pull off the shelf to do stuff, and to avoid doing the dumb things again, because somebody already did the dumb thing and wrote about their experience and we don't need to do it again. There are several different processes that are creating that record, and other processes where people are trying to destroy bits of that record, and others that are trying to prevent people from putting things into that record in the first place. We all live off that intellectual record. So what we want to do is get as much into the record, prevent as much as possible being deleted from the record, and then make the record as searchable as possible.

ES: But one consequence of this view is that actors will find the generation of very large amounts of misinformation strategic for them.

JA: Yes. This is another type of censorship that I have thought about but don't speak so much about, which is censorship through complexity.

ES: Right. Too complicated.

JA: And that is basically the offshore financial sector. Censorship through complexity. Censorship of what? Censorship of political outrage. With enough political outrage there is law reform and if there's law reform you can't do it anymore. So why is it that all these careful tax-structuring arrangements are so complex? They may be perfectly legal, but why are they so goddamn complex? Well, because the ones that weren't complex were understood, and the ones that were understood were regulated, so you're only left with the things that are incredibly complex.

SM: More noise, less signal kind of thing.

JA: Yes, exactly.

ES: But how in the future will people deal with the fact that the incentive to publish information that is misleading, wrong, manipulative, is very high? Furthermore, you can't figure out who the bad publisher was as well as the good, because there's anonymity in the system.

JA: First we must understand that the way it is right now is very bad. A journalist for the *Nation*, Greg Mitchell, who has also written about us, wrote a book about the mainstream media called *So Wrong for So Long*.[229] And that title is basically it. Yes we have these heroic moments with Watergate and so on, but actually, come on, the press has never been very good. It has always been very bad. Fine journalists are an exception to the rule. When you are involved in something yourself, like I am with WikiLeaks, and you know every facet of it, you look to see what is reported about it in the mainstream press and you see naked lie after naked lie. You know that the journalist knows it's a lie; it is not a simple mistake. Then people repeat lies and so on. The condition of the mainstream press nowadays is so appalling I don't think it can be reformed. I don't think that is possible. I think it has to be eliminated, and replaced with something that's better.

SM: Which does seem to be happening!

JA: Yes, and I have been pushing this idea of scientific journalism—that things must be precisely cited with the original source, and as much of the information as possible should be put in the public domain so that people can look at it, just like in science so that you can test to see whether the conclusion follows from the experimental data.[230] Otherwise the journalist probably just made it up. In fact, that is what happens all the time: people just make it up. They make it up to such a degree that we are led to war. Most wars in the twentieth century started as a result

---

229. Greg Mitchell, *So Wrong for So Long: How the Press, the Pundits—and the President—Failed on Iraq* (Union Square Press, 2008).

230. There is more discussion of this idea in Raffi Khatchadourian, "No Secrets: Julian Assange's mission for total transparency," *New Yorker*, 7 June 2010, archive.today/zZYqJ

of lies amplified and spread by the mainstream press. And you may say, "Well that is a horrible circumstance; it is terrible that all these wars start with lies." And I say no, this is a tremendous opportunity, because it means that populations basically don't like wars and they have to be lied into it. That means we can be "truthed" into peace. That is cause for great hope.

But this question of how you distinguish truthful publishers from untruthful publishers is a reputational business. What I would like to see is the introduction to journalism of that part of the reputational business, as in science, that asks, "Where is your data?" If you're not providing your data why the hell should I take this seriously? Now that we can publish on the internet, now that there is physically room for the data, it should be there. Newspapers don't have physical room for the primary source; now that there is physical room for the primary source we should create a standard that it should be there. People can deviate from this standard, but if they deviate from the standard and can't be bothered to provide us with the primary source data then why should we pay any attention to what they are writing? They are not treating the reader with respect.

I guess the issue of reputation is an important issue, actually. How do things have a reputation? Part of the way that they have a reputation is through a series of citations. Something happens, someone else says something about it, someone else says something about that, and so on. This is a series of citations as information flows from one person to another. For that to be strong you need a strong naming system, where what you are relying on is not some startup website that disappears tomorrow, or one that is modifying information because a company doesn't like it, or one that has been sued out of existence. That, I think, would help with reputation.

Complexity is harder. I think that is a big problem. When things become open they tend to become more complex because people start hiding what they are doing—their bad behavior—through complexity. An example is bureaucratic doublespeak. Things get bureaucratized and everything becomes mealymouthed. That's a cost of openness. In the offshore sector you see incredible complexity in the layers of things happening so they become impenetrable. Of course cryptography is an intellectual system that has specialized in making things as complex as possible. Those things are hard to attack. On the other hand, complex systems are also hard to use. Bureaucracies and internal communication systems that are full of weasel words and ass covering are inefficient internal communication systems. Similarly, those tremendously complex offshore structuring arrangements are actually inefficient. Maybe you're ahead when the tax regime is high, but if the tax regime is 3 percent, you're not going to be ahead at all; you're going to be choked by the complexity.

SM: Well, if they weren't inefficient then everybody would have their money offshore, Julian.

JA: Yes, that's right.

SM: I meant that as a joke, but it's probably true.

JA: No, that's true. There's a battle between all of these things going on. I don't see a difference between government and big corporations and small corporations. This is all one continuum; these are all systems that are trying to get as much power as possible. A general is trying to get as much power for his section of the army, and so on. They advertise, they produce something that they claim is a product, people buy it, people don't buy it, they complexify in order to hide the flaws in their product, and they spin. So I don't see a big difference between government and nongovernment actors in that way. There is one theoretical difference concerning the ability to deploy coercive force, but even there we see that well-connected corporations are able to tap into the government or courts and are consequently able to deploy coercive force by sending police to do debt requisition or kick employees out of the office.

SECRECY IS CRIMINOGENIC

SM: Can I just ask you about the same thing but sort of in reverse, which is the ways in which the sources of information as individuals can and can't be protected? In other words, how can their information be anonymous, so that they don't pay a price for circulating it? Maybe with one example from North Korea or Iran and one example from the US, and the differences between those two scenarios.

JA: There are many ways for people to transmit things anonymously. One of the greatest difficulties for sources is their proximity to the material. If they have high proximity to the material and there is a limited number of people that know it, it actually doesn't matter what technical mechanism you then apply; it would be quite difficult for them to evade scrutiny and it doesn't matter what country or regime they are in. But systematic injustice by definition is going to have to involve many people. So while maybe you cannot safely get records out of the inner sanctum of cabinet, if those decisions are to produce some unjust consequence which affects many people, then a lot of people inside must see at least the shadow of secret high-level planning as the instructions for implementation start spreading down to lower levels. Maybe the whole plan isn't visible by the time it gets down to the grunts, but its components must be.

This struck me when we got hold of the two main manuals for Guantánamo Bay. The 2003 manual was the first one obtained, written by Major General Geoffrey Miller, who subsequently went over to Abu Ghraib to "Gitmo-ize" it, as Donald Rumsfeld called it.[231] That manual had all sorts of abuses in it.[232] One that I was surprised to see was an explicit instruction to falsify records for the Red Cross. How many people had read this manual? All the prison captains at Guantánamo Bay had. Why would you risk telling the grunts this sort of information? It wasn't even classified; they made it unclassified—"For Official Use Only"—why? Because it's more expensive to get people who have classification clearance. If you hire contractors without classification clearance it's cheaper. You can't whisper to the coalface.[233] You can't have the president whispering to the coalface because the coalface is too big. You can't have the president whispering to the intermediaries because then you end up with Chinese whispers and that means your instructions aren't carried out. So if you take information off paper, outside of the electronic or physical paper trail, instructions decay. And that's why

---

231. Geoffrey Miller is the United States army major general who commanded the US detention facilities at Guantánamo Bay (Gitmo) and Abu Ghraib in Iraq.

    Donald Rumsfeld was the US secretary of defense from 2001 to 2006 (and previously from 1975 to 1977).

232. "Camp Delta Standard Operating Procedure," WikiLeaks, 7 November 2007, archive.today/P9HMH

    See also Julian Assange, Daniel Mathews, with Emi Maclean, Marc Falkoff, Rebecca Dick, and Beth Gilson (habeas counsel), "Changes in Guantanamo Bay SOP manual (2003–2004)," WikiLeaks, 3 December 2007, archive.today/b3A1g

233. The "coalface" refers to those closest to the front line. It was originally a reference to miners who removed coal from the face of the mine.

all organizations of any scale have rigorous paper trails for the instructions from the leadership. But by definition if you are trying to get a lot of people to do something you are going to have to have instructions, which means there is always going to be a paper trail. Small-group decisions that don't end up going to the coalface are an exception. But if these small-group decisions don't go to the coalface and instruct many people, are they so important in the scheme of things?

SM: Right, they're going to be ineffective.

ES: We went to Berlin, there's the place where they signed the final order, what's it called?

LS: Final Solution. Wannsee.[234]

ES: Wannsee, and these are Germans so they documented everything.

LS: It's fascinating.

ES: So it's exactly your point. In order to kill six million Jews, you have to actually write it down.

JA: It's a big logistical process.

ES: Absolutely, and many, many things need to be communicated, what the procedures were and so on, and here are the pictures of people and their signatures and so forth.

---

234. The Wannsee Conference was a meeting of senior Nazi officials at which the implementation of the "Final Solution" was coordinated, in which millions of Jews from German-occupied Europe were exterminated in concentration camps.

LS: Minutes of the meeting.

ES: It was like, seriously chilling. This is the banality of evil.[235]

LS: Indeed.

JA: Yes, but this is one of the first internal arguments I had with other people in 2006. They would say, "Well, okay, you have a good get, you can expose some organization and show it has been abusing something in some way, and it will just take everything off paper and use oral instructions." And I said, "No, that's not going to happen, because if it does go that way, if they take everything off paper, if they internally balkanize so that information can't be leaked, they will incur a tremendous cost to their organizational efficiency. And if, nonetheless, they were to do that, it would mean that this abusive organization would simply become less powerful in its struggle for economic equilibrium and political equilibrium with all other organizations."

ES: This is the inverse of your argument about empowering the dissidents in Egypt. They needed SMS to communicate. In your argument, by stopping the inability to coordinate at this level, the inverse of your argument. Literally the inverse of the first argument. Your argument would be if you take those tools away. . . .

---

235. The phrase "banality of evil" is from *Eichmann in Jerusalem: A Report on the Banality of Evil* by political theorist Hannah Arendt. The phrase has come to refer to the unthinking banality often seen in systematized inhumanity, which seems to arise from abstraction, indirection, habituation, or other normalization processes.

JA: Yes, well, I say they take them away themselves. There are all sorts of reasons why non-powerful organizations engage in secrecy, which to my view is legitimate; they need it, because they are powerless. But why do powerful organizations engage in secrecy? Well, usually it's because if the plans that they have are made public, the public would oppose them. Plans that are opposed before implementation often don't get implemented, so they want to wait as long as possible before going public. Implementation eventually makes the plans public by the very fact that they are being implemented, but by then it is too late to alter the course of the actions effectively.

On the other hand, an organization that is engaged in planning behavior that would not be opposed by the public doesn't have that burden. It doesn't have to take things off paper. So this will be an efficient organization; the other one will be an inefficient organization. In the mix, as they do economic and political battle, the efficient organization will grow and the inefficient one will shrink.

ES: Is that your fundamental justification, do you think, for what you're doing?

JA: There are really two fundamental justifications. First of all, human civilization, its good part, is based upon our full intellectual record, and our intellectual record should be as large as possible if humanity is to be as advanced as possible. The second is that, in practice, releasing information is positive to those engaged in acts that the public supports and negative to those engaged in acts that the public does not support.

ES: So it's a form of restraint.

JA: It can create a redress for an act of injustice that is revealed. That's nice. But the larger effect is that it creates disincentives for organizations that create unjust plans or engage in unjust acts.

ES: One more follow-up question. In ten years, what does this world look like? In other words, if you extrapolate this argument.

JA: Well, we are at a bit of a crossroads, no? It could go either way.

SM: What about an optimistic scenario and a pessimistic scenario?

JA: Remember Philip Zimmermann's PGP case?

ES: Yes.

JA: That was just a grand jury investigation. It was moderately serious, but he wasn't convicted. No one at that time was even charged; they were being investigated. It changed the behavior of tens of thousands of people who were involved in choosing whether to put cryptography into programs or not.[236] All sorts

---

236. This is a reference to the "cryptowars" of the 1990s. When cypherpunk activists began to spread strong cryptographic tools as free software, the US administration took steps to prevent cryptographic tools being used effectively. It classified cryptography as a munition and restricted its export; it tried to introduce competing technologies that were deliberately broken so that law enforcement and intelligence agencies could always decrypt information; and it tried to introduce the controversial "key escrow" scheme. For a short period after the turn of the century it was widely accepted that these efforts had been comprehensively defeated. However, a "second cryptowar" is now well underway, with legislative, technical, and covert efforts to backdoor or otherwise marginalize the use of cryptography.

of tortured copyright assignments and inter-software company structuring arrangements were engaged in, just from that negative signal of a grand jury investigation. Signals about what behavior is acceptable, what behavior you can get away with, what behavior is beneficial to individuals engaged in it and what behavior is not change how many people behave.

We are at a crossroads now where those organizations that are fighting against those people who want to be able to publish freely and disclose important information to the public . . . I can't remember the beginning of this sentence now.

JC: You said we are at a crossroads now where those organizations that are fighting against those people who want to be able to publish freely and disclose important information to the public.

JA: It was pretty tortured wasn't it? Okay, ha. We are at a crossroads now where those organizations that are fighting against those people who want to be able to publish freely and disclose important information to the public could produce, if successful, a signal which discourages almost everyone from engaging in those activities. Or we, and people who share our values, could be successful and that will become the new norm of accepted behavior.

SM: And what are the necessary conditions for that to occur, the latter? I can easily imagine the necessary conditions for the former.

JA: Everyone gives money to WikiLeaks!

[*Laughter*]

SM: Are you taking Bitcoin?

JA: Yes! It's interesting to know whether, if people read this and then act, their action will be enough to change the result. That is why we are at a very interesting period. I think we are literally at this crossroads and a little bit more of a push to one direction or another could change the outcome a lot. So if people want to see the values that we promote succeed, they should promote those organizations and individuals that represent those values, and start taking it on themselves.

SM: I was going to say, or become it.

JA: Yes, become it. Become representations of those values themselves. I am always hesitant in saying that everyone should go out and become a martyr. I don't believe that. I believe the most effective activists are those that fight and run away to fight another day, not those who fight and martyr themselves. That's about judgment—when to engage in the fight and when to withdraw so as to preserve your resources for the next fight.

JC: Would you make the argument that physically fighting and running away is not that different from fighting anonymously, so long as you are sufficiently confident that your anonymity is strong?

JA: If you have perfect anonymity you can fight forever, yes. You don't have to run away.

SM: You've pre–run away

[*Laughter*]

JC: That's it in essence. Pre–running away.

JA: You can lower the courage threshold. That's one of the nice things that anonymity does. Maybe that's not the right way to put it. People often say, "You are tremendously courageous in doing what you're doing." And I say, "No, you misunderstand what courage is. Courage is not the absence of fear. Only fools have no fear. Rather, courage is the intellectual mastery of fear by understanding the true risks and opportunities of the situation and keeping those things in balance." It is not simply having prejudice about what the risks are, but actually testing them. There are all sorts of myths that go around about what can be done and what cannot be done. It's important to test. You don't test by jumping off a bridge. You test by jumping off a footstool, and then jumping off something a bit higher and a bit higher.

JC: Can I just ask a follow-up to that? It goes back to what Scott was asking about the relationship between the person providing information and the person receiving it. If we look at all the different societies around the world, presumably not everyone is starting on the same level playing field. There are some people that just have a greater education of the risks associated with using these tools. There are some people who are going to provide information in societies where the governments aren't as vigilant, and some where they are very vigilant. It would seem that in a place like an Iran or a North Korea, where the combination of very vigilant regimes, with populations that are still relatively new to these tools and the risks associated with them, may not be able to actually have that understanding of the true risks of the situation, and the opportunities that you were mentioning.

JA: I think they're capable of learning, like everyone else. These societies are much more political than the West. People like to talk about politics over dinner every night. So I am not sure it is right to take this Western eye and think that these people don't understand the lot that they are in. The extrinsic risks might be higher; the other risks associated with conducting a political life may already be quite high. So one has to keep these risks in proportion. Also the potential rewards are much greater. One might be involved in a very grand historic moment and become swept up in it. And because we all only live once, we all suffer the continuous risk of not having lived our life well. Every year that is not used is 100 percent wasted.

ES: Here's an aside for you. I was with Warren Buffett, who's 78. And I said, "What are you up to?" And he said, "This next year will be the best year of my life." And I said, "Okay . . ." He's obviously playing with me. And then I figured it out that if you're 76 then the next year is going to be the best year of the rest of your life. Because at some point there is going to be a year where it's not going to be so good. And then you are going to be dead. And so, I love that, right? This next is going to be the best year.

[*Laughter*]

LS: Julian, how do you feel about photographs for the book? Do you mind if I take snapshots of you guys just working? How do you? You can see them. Up to you. I would just take shots this way, and then that way.

JA: Of who doing what, exactly?

LS: Of you guys talking. Just conversation.

JA: Oh, that's all right.

ES: Using my S95 camera

LS: Yes. Exactly, it's a very high-tech operation going on here.

JA: Just don't say anything anti-Semitic for the next few months!

ES: We would never say anything anti-Semitic.

JA: No, no, it's just that this Russian journalist came over and took a photo with me. His name is Israel Shamir, he is as Jewish as could possibly be, but he converted to Russian Orthodox, and is very anti-Judaism. He then put this out in *Russian Reporter* or something with this photo with me, and I started to cop it in the most unbelievable way.

ES: Interesting. You and I both understand the costs of negative publicity.

JA: It's just a joke. I know you have been well tested.

ES: I am very well tested. I am very well behaved. The criticism that is constant is that damage has occurred because of WikiLeaks. I can't find it yet. Do you have a reasoned . . . ?

JA: Well, it's a rhetorical trick.

ES: You understand why I'm asking the question?

JA: Yeah, yeah.

ES: I'm trying to understand the case against your vision, which obviously we are sympathetic to.

JA: Up until Collateral Murder we were a cause célèbre in the United States among various groups; actually we are still a cause célèbre, but it is in a smaller left-wing or libertarian right-wing community now.[237] According to Reuters, across twenty-four countries we have the support of over three-quarters of the general population. Our support is worst in the United States, where we have the support of over 40 percent of the population, which is still pretty good considering what has been happening.

As a result of embarrassing the US military and diplomatic class, we have had a counterattack. That counterattack is significant. This is a very significant power group that is not just at the top of the White House, it's not just a few generals; rather, it is all the people connected to and profiting from that system. That's about a third of the US population, all the way from Chelsea Clinton to someone in the gutters of San Antonio whose brother is deployed in Iraq. There are 900,000 people in the United States with top-secret security clearances at this moment.[238] There are two and a half million that have

---

237. Collateral Murder is a video published by WikiLeaks showing US military helicopter footage from Iraq of the indiscriminate killing of civilians, including two Reuters journalists. At the time of writing it has been viewed more than 14 million times on YouTube. "Collateral Murder – WikiLeaks – Iraq" (video), uploaded 3 April 2010, youtu.be/5rXPrfnU3G0

238. The figure was reported in July 2010 as 854,000. See Dana Priest, William M. Arkin, "A hidden world, growing beyond control," *Washington Post*, 19 July 2010, archive.today/3C0wq

By 2014 this had increased to 1.5 million. See Brian Fung, "5.1 million Americans have security clearances. That's more than the entire population of Norway," *Washington Post*, 24 March 2014, archive.today/46So6

classified security clearances.[239] If we go back over the past twenty years and ask how many people had security clearances, maybe it is 15 million. If we then go and look at all their spouses and business partners and children we are looking at something like 30 percent of the population of the United States that is one degree removed from that ideological structure and that patronage system. It is quite difficult in the United States to say something that is against that system. The *New York Times* has found that to its peril when it tried to speak out against it. When it published material from WikiLeaks it had to react very defensively. Even traditional US journalists think that it is sickening to see a newspaper of any strength saying how "pleased" the White House was with its behavior.[240]

If we look at the attacks on us, they always use the words "placed people at risk." But risk relative to what? Right now we are at risk of a meteorite passing through the roof of this house and killing us all. That is a risk, it is true, but is it a risk that is significant enough to be

---

239. At the time of the conversation in 2011, 2.5 million was a current figure, dating from a 2009 Government Accountability Office report. See Steven Aftergood, "More Than 2.4 Million Hold Security Clearances," *Secrecy News*, 29 July 2009, archive.today/kThm8

   However, by September 2011, new figures had emerged, bumping the figure to 4.2 million. See Steven Aftergood, "Number of Security Clearances Soars," *Secrecy News*, 20 September 2011, archive.today/Hw6x2

   As of 2014, the figure had risen to 5.1 million, a state within a state, with a population greater than that of Norway. See Brian Fung, "5.1 million Americans have security clearances. That's more than the entire population of Norway," *Washington Post*, 24 March 2014, archive.today/46So6

240. For example, the *New York Times* boasted that the White House "thanked us for handling the documents with care." "The War Logs Articles," *New York Times*, 25 July 2010, archive.today/a2lVO

worth speaking about? The answer is no. It is similar with the word "possibility." There is a possibility that a meteorite could descend on us all in this moment, but it is not a probability. People who are making an argument in relation to security often use these rhetorical tricks—there is a risk of something; there is a possibility of something. People need to engage in an intellectual defense against this manipulation by rhetoric, by understanding that if someone mentions that there's a risk without saying that the risk is higher than crossing the road, or twice that of being stung by a bee, then you must ignore it. Similarly with possibility versus probability.

ES: Yeah, I can do all this in my head too. Are there examples where a positive outcome could be directly traced to WikiLeaks in the political sphere that you would want to highlight? Something that is a specific tangible positive outcome?

JA: The most significant one seems to be the Arab Spring.

ES: You would argue that WikiLeaks was out there—

JA: Amnesty International did in its latest report and Tunisian activists and academics did.[241] Because of my direct involvement it would

---

241. *Amnesty International Report 2011: The state of the world's human rights* (report), Amnesty International, May 2011, pp. xiv–xvi, is.gd/C4JNVP

See also "WikiLeaks: The secret life of a superpower" Episode 1 (documentary), BBC, first broadcast 21 March 2012, archive.today/pKuQZ. In lieu of a transcript, the subtitles of the program are available from Amara: archive.today/uak1V

See also "Deconstructing Tunileaks: An Interview with Professor Rob Prince, University of Denver," *Nawaat*, 20 December 2010, archive.today/5TiD4

be unseemly for me to argue that directly, and I am not certain about it directly. I am certain that we affected it and we were deeply involved in it.

ES: Influenced it.

JA: I am certain that we influenced it. And that is really something of great moment. Something I am certain about is that we changed the outcome of the Kenyan election in 2007.[242] There have been many ministers whose scalps we've taken and people being forced to resign and so on. Those are concrete and clear actions. One might argue that they were positive if one didn't like the guy, and one would argue that they were negative if one did like the guy, so I don't really want to mention those ones.

ES: Yes, if I go back to your earlier argument that the effect on a single individual is not your actual goal. The actual effect is to change the system in some fundamental way, because you make

---

See also Lina Ben Mhenni, "Tunisia: Censorship Continues as WikiLeaks Cables Make the Rounds," *Global Voices Advocacy*, 7 December 2010, archive.today/MW9aR

242. "The looting of Kenya under President Moi," WikiLeaks, 30 August 2007, updated 9 September 2007, archive.today/JdHZ4

See also "Kenyan Presidential Election, 2007," *Wikipedia*, archive.today/TEj60

See also "2007–08 Kenyan Crisis," *Wikipedia*, archive.today/Rgg1g

See also "Corruption in Kenya," *Wikipedia*, archive.today/b7ve8

See also Xan Rice, "The looting of Kenya," *Guardian*, 31 August 2007, archive.today/VR7V1

See also Nick Wadhams, "Kenyan President Moi's 'corruption' laid bare," *Telegraph*, 1 September 2007, archive.today/KxkB1

See also Barney Jopson, "Kenya graft in spotlight," *Financial Times*, 31 August 2007, archive.today/k2t0i

the argument that these systems have become fiscalized, they are static, independent of any pressure, so an example of a truly large influence would be a revolution. Right?

JA: Yes, well, you can have a large influence without these dichotomic events, but the dichotomic events—binary events—are easy to talk about and are provable.

ES: It's also a marketing prop. You want to have a marketing story.

JA: One party or another party wins the election and it changed. That is a very clear outcome. There is a revolution; one group is in power, and then another group is in power. That is a very clear change. I suspect some of the other changes we have influenced are more significant. I suspect the liberalization of the publishing environment is the most significant change that we have been involved in, and something we have pushed for many years.[243] There is no way that what we did last year we could have done four years ago; it would not have been possible.

ES: How come? Technologically? Or in terms of—

---

243. WikiLeaks has campaigned for a liberalized publishing environment for as long as it has existed. Besides the practical demonstration of the freedom of expression, WikiLeaks' most notable contributions have been the release of internet censorship blacklists and its founding advisory role in the Icelandic Modern Media Initiative. See "Internet Censorship," WikiLeaks, archive.today/EfZ6g

See also Julian Assange, "WikiLeaks editor: why I'm excited about Iceland's plans for journalism," *Guardian*, 15 February 2010, archive.today/lK3u2

See also Chris Vallance, "WikiLeaks and Iceland MPs propose 'journalism haven,'" BBC, 12 February 2010, archive.today/cOjgM

See also the International Modern Media Institute: www.immi.is

JA: Technologically it was all perfectly possible. The difference is a shift in the status quo: WikiLeaks became the status quo. That wasn't always so. During the first two years we were battling over whether we were even acceptable on the internet. Then there was the Bank Julius Baer case, where we were involved in a big legal case in San Francisco.[244] On the one hand there was us, and on the other hand there was the largest private Swiss banking concern Bank Julius Baer, which was trying to shut us down. We conclusively won, and cost them their US IPO as a result.[245]

---

244. Bank Julius Baer (BJB) was the largest Swiss private banking group. In 2008, WikiLeaks posted documents exposing massive tax evasion committed by individuals and corporations associated with BJB, involving trust accounts held in the Cayman Islands. The banking group responded by obtaining a court injunction on Dynadot, WikiLeaks' Californian domain name registrar. This move provoked public outcry, and the injunction was soon overturned after a coalition of publishers, including the Associated Press, filed an amicus brief with the court. BJB eventually dropped its case. See Bank Julius Baer & Co. Ltd. Et al v. WikiLeaks et al, JUSTIA Dockets & Filings, archive.today/BEaNB

See also "Full correspondence between WikiLeaks and Bank Julius Baer," WikiLeaks, 19 February 2008, archive.today/3k3Lf

See also Kim Zetter, "Cayman Islands Bank Gets WikiLeaks Taken Offline in U.S.—Updated with Links," *Wired*, 18 February 2008, archive.today/vND8k

245. Soon after its failed attempt to censor WikiLeaks, Bank Julius Baer canceled its scheduled US IPO (initial public stock offer). See the Securities and Exchange Commission, Form S-1, Julius Baer Americas Inc., 6282 (Primary Standard Industrial Classification Code Number), archive.today/WaUt1

See also Christopher Condon, "Baer to Sell Up to $1 Billion in U.S. Fund Unit (Update3)," *Bloomberg*, 12 February 2008, archive.today/cowj2

See also Richard Koman, "Bank that censored WikiLeaks was preparing for IPO," *ZDNet*, 20 February 2008, archive.today/r2rur

That sent out a signal that there is a place in the world for a publisher like WikiLeaks, and we started to cement that place as time went by. And now we have really cemented it because in October 2010 the Pentagon stood up in public and gave a forty-minute press conference with their spokesperson, Geoff Morrell, saying that WikiLeaks must—and I personally must—return everything that we had ever published that had been derived from the Pentagon, return everything that we were going to publish, and cease soliciting information from US military or government personnel, or the Pentagon would compel us to do so. When asked by a journalist at the press conference what mechanisms they had to compel us, the response was, "Well, look, this is the Pentagon; we are not concerned about the law."[246]

JC: When you watched that did you get the impression that they were just an unbelievable level of naïveté or lack of understanding about the actual technology or technical aspects of this that would make that impossible?

JA: I did, but then later on I developed a more sophisticated understanding of what was going on in that press conference.

JC: I usually start out very unsophisticated. Ha-ha-ha.

---

246. See the transcript of the press conference. "DOD News Briefing with Geoff Morrell from the Pentagon" (transcript), US Department of Defense, 5 August 2010, archive.today/nHyaW

The press conference can also be viewed on YouTube. "Pentagon Press Conference re: WikiLeaks Part 1 of 4" (video), uploaded 26 September 2010, youtu.be/DJe_Q8XFIHI

JA: What was actually going on? It seems ridiculous. Why would the Pentagon act like a victim? Why would they look so ridiculous and powerless? Why would they give a demand that they were not capable of fulfilling? It would make them look weak. But it was a carefully constructed legal message, designed to embroil us in the US Espionage Act. It was a notification, like you see in the newspapers.

ES: Yeah.

JA: We demand that you do this. This is the type of information that will cause grave harm to US national security. We hold a press conference so that we can argue that all those WikiLeaks people have seen it. Then the next thing WikiLeaks publishes will demonstrate intent. Despite the fact that WikiLeaks has been informed, they did it anyway; therefore they have intent, because you can't accidentally commit espionage.

SM: That's why they are concerned with the past and not just the present. Because there has to be a pattern of practice and as long as it's instances of fresh incidents then there's no pattern.

JA: Yes, but we said no, quickly, before we had understood what the legal trap was. Then in relatively short order we produced the Iraqi War Diaries, which is one of the best things we've ever done.[247]

[*Tape paused*]

---

247. The Iraq War Diaries, WikiLeaks, 22 October 2010, warlogs.wikileaks.org

INTERLUDE

[*Recording resumes in another room*]

SM: . . . increasingly using WikiLeaks information as a source, sometimes done without even mentioning that it was a source.

JA: Well, in the beginning they wouldn't cite WikiLeaks as the source; now they do. It gives them more prestige now to say that it came from us.

SM: I know, I know, I know.

JA: Funny, isn't it?

SM: It is, it is, it is.

JA: I'll just show you something funny. Do you like our slogan?

ES: Keep calm and carry on, ha-ha-ha.

SM: The Second World War!

ES: We were admiring the pictures of all of the owner's ancestors.

JA: These are Vaughan's ancestors. That's Vaughan there, my friend. That's from Afghanistan earlier this year.

ES: He's a sort of reporter type, right?

JA: He's a war reporter.

SM: I'm sorry, who is this?

JA: This is the owner of the house, my friend, Vaughan Smith.

SM: Oh, right, right. I've been to his club![248]

JA: Yes, he's a war reporter. Although he was in the Grenadier Guards originally, and then I think he understood that you could go to more wars as a war reporter than as a soldier.

SM: Ha-ha-ha. And different ones. It's better that way. This is his family?

JA: These are all family. That's his father and mother and they both live here in a house on the edge of the estate.

JC: So it's a military family from a little ways back.

JA: The other interesting guy is that guy right there, Tiger Smith, the rakish looking one with the collar up, who is famous for killing 99 tigers back when that sort of thing was approved of. Saving Indians.

JC: So he was a Raj figure of some kind?

---

248. The club being referred to is the Frontline Club, a popular member's club for war reporters and journalists in London's Paddington area. The club was the venue for several of WikiLeaks' most high-profile press conferences. www.frontlineclub.com

JA: Yes. Here is the comedy part. Vaughan's father was the Queen's messenger.

LS: Oh, Elizabeth.

JA: He would go on airplanes and deliver messages. Now, see this bag in his hand there? You know what's in this bag?

SM: State secrets.

JA: Diplomatic cables!

[*Laughter*]

ES: That's great.

JA: He would go on the Concorde, and have a seat to the left and a seat to the right filled with cable bags and deliveries. Sometimes he would take computers as well. People would come into the bay of the airplane to guide it in and make sure they weren't stolen, and other guys would be waiting at the other end to take them.

LS: And what does he say about it?

JA: He's sort of horrified on the one hand and deeply pleased on the other, because if they had just used him none of this would have happened!

[*Laughter*]

ES: And let me just ask, you've been here for about six months?

JA: Eight months.

ES: So this is your home.

SM: Well, it's a lovely place.

JA: I have to go to the police station every day.

ES: How far is it to the police station?

JA: About fifteen, twenty minutes. I am frequently ambushed. A woman from Catalonia was the most amusing. She turned up at the Frontline Club in London and tried to convince them that she was WikiLeaks' star Spanish programmer.

ES: Ha-ha-ha-ha-ha!

JA: And of course not knowing anything about programming, she just gave some technobabble and they assumed it was true. And then after a while they were like, "Uh, well, you can't really see Julian, he's in seclusion." They put her up for free for one night. She had this habit of listening in on a bit of a conversation and then reincorporating it into her story. And the next day: "Oh, I know this person; oh look, there's so-and-so."

ES: Ha-ha-ha.

JA: Then two weeks later I'm here and the police come to the door, and they say, "Do you know X?"

"X? X who?"

"Your fiancée!"

[*Laughter*]

"No, no?"

"Well she stayed at a house on the edge of this property all night and she says that you are going to pay the taxi bill."

[*Gasps*]

And I'm like, "What taxi bill?" It turns out that she had come from Catalonia to London, got a black cab from London to here—500 pounds; she had 50 pounds. She convinced the taxi driver that her "rich, famous" fiancé would pay for it, they were just in a bit of a dispute at the moment but it would be sorted out in the morning. Then she had gone to the edge of the property and convinced them that she was my fiancée, and the taxi driver wouldn't go because he wanted his money. The people at the edge of the property put them both up for the night.

[*Laughter*]

SM: At what point do you just pay her for the creativity?

[*Laughter*]

ES: For the entertainment!

SM: It's so creative, it's almost impressive.

ES: I want to be sensitive to your energy and time. I think it would be interesting to talk a bit about the various what-if scenarios. That's what we're very interested in; Jared and I do this all the time. What are some scenarios that could play out? You know, try to actually think about it. You've all these different actors and players, and you obviously think about it, you're basically a physicist, right. You think about it that way.

JA: Maybe we should go for a walk, then.

IT'S NOT EASY TO DO A WIKILEAKS

[*Walking on stones*]

JC: In thinking about what-if scenarios it can actually be useful to think "what if" in the past. Like when we were sitting there, one of our chapters looks at intervention in the context of a futuristic genocide, but I think it is actually a more useful conversation in terms of understanding the role that WikiLeaks could play in a situation like that to ask, in 1994, had the technological stage of the world today been the technological state then, and WikiLeaks was around during the Rwanda genocide, what might have changed?[249] How might things have been different?

JA: I'm just wondering if the weather will change.

JC: Welcome to British weather. Ha-ha.

ES: Well, you know, the cloud will move.

JA: The Rwandan genocide. Yes, I think it would have been a bit different if they had internet and a number of phones in Rwanda; I think the message would have come out more. Although maybe not

---

249. In 1994, over approximately 100 days, Hutus slaughtered 500,000 to 1 million Tutsis, representing up to 20 percent of Rwanda's total population.

that much: all the bad things happening now in Congo aren't really getting much traction in the West.

[*Rain*]

SM: That's a fantastic tree. It'll keep us totally dry.

JA: That's good.

JC: There is a larger what-if question here. It is part what if, and part why. Like why haven't there been people in places like Iran or North Korea or Congo releasing documents in the same way as there have been in, say, in Western democracies.

JA: Well, we have got a bit of material from Iran, actually.[250] It's not that easy to do a WikiLeaks—the combination of technicalities, reputation, and funding and so on. It's not that easy to do.

SM: Reputation is not easy to do, for one thing.

ES: Okay, but let's ask the question bluntly. Why are you not getting enormous numbers of anonymous USB drives about the bad documents in African countries that are run by these evil dictator types?

JA: We have.

ES: Don't you think that everyone would be incentivized to use you? Shouldn't they be?

---

250. For example, see "Assorted plans and papers from the Iranian Ammunition Industries Group, 2009," WikiLeaks, 17 July 2009, archive.today/Ycl1m

See also Julian Assange, "Serious nuclear accident may lay behind Iranian nuke chief's mystery resignation," WikiLeaks, 17 July 2009, archive.today/wCbof

JA: We have got some decent African stuff. Decent East Timorese stuff. Lots of decent Latin American stuff.[251]

ES: Is it because these governments don't write down as much of this stuff?

JA: They are not as networked. Some of them don't use English as their governmental language. The Tanzanian government uses Kiswahili. A lot of it is to do with whether they perceive WikiLeaks as a political actor within their country. Once we started doing a little bit of East Timor, we got a lot more of East Timor, and then a flood opened up, and it became routine for them to give us material. But they need to perceive that we are part of the community. For Russia, although now we have RuLeaks, which has been doing pretty well, I think the small amount of material that we have released is actually a positive sign, in that the Russian internet sphere is very vibrant.[252]

ES: Yeah, I was just there; it's amazing.

JA: It doesn't look outside so much. Why would it look at an English-language website like WikiLeaks? It has its nonprofit activist journalists and opposition and they are all in that internet sphere, which is relatively free compared to Russian TV. So they don't see that they really need this other avenue.

---

251. WikiLeaks' publications can be browsed by country at:
    www.wikileaks.org/wiki/Category:Countries
       For examples from African countries, see WikiLeaks: archive.today/reC33
       For examples from East Timor, see WikiLeaks: archive.today/vQtYO

252. RuLeaks: www.ruleaks.net

There was the publication of a whole load of FSB documents, on an American server, which was then immediately hacked and taken down and never seen again.[253] It's not so easy to publish against powerful state actors.

JC: You've talked a lot about the importance of the name; it has been an important theme in this conversation. There's the debut, in which the site goes live, then there's the major debut where it becomes a household term or a household name, and one of the things that we are playing around with in the book—

JA: We haven't properly used that yet, though. We haven't been able to grow as fast as the name has been able to grow.

JC: People know what WikiLeaks is, and I wonder had the first batch of documents that you received been from say an Iran or from a North Korea and released, if the world would have looked at it as a whistleblowing platform?

JA: It did![254] The world did up until we started producing a high volume of US military stuff. We were producing thousands of pages of US military stuff back in 2007.[255]

---

253. The FSB is the Federal Security Service of the Russian Federation, the successor to the KGB.

254. WikiLeaks' first publications in 2006 were from Somalia, and concerned the Somali Union of Islamic Courts. Some of the documents around this leak were sourced from China. See WikiLeaks: archive.today/ewGbU
   See also "Inside Somalia and the Union of Islamic Courts," WikiLeaks, archive.today/emqVb

255. See WikiLeaks' list of publications for the year 2007: archive.today/zER02

ES: And nobody noticed.

JC: That's interesting.

ES: Because the Collateral Damage video wasn't out there.

JA: People noticed the Guantánamo stuff, but not to the extent that WikiLeaks became a household name. We were a journalistic name pretty quickly. And in the techno part of the human rights community we were a name pretty quickly. And we were a name in the internet-educated German- and English-speaking publics, especially toward the crypto-security end. For example, when we did a fundraising effort from the beginning of 2010 to March 2010, before Collateral Murder, we raised a million bucks. For a new—new in terms of concept—nonprofit journalism group to raise a million bucks in twenty-dollar donations is almost completely unheard of. We were doing that before Collateral Murder.

Not even Collateral Murder made us into a worldwide name. It made us into a US household name. All these things started to stack up by the end of the year. Really it was the Pentagon's attack against us, and the Swedish sex case, funnily enough, that made us into a worldwide household name with 84 percent name recognition worldwide.[256]

---

256. The figure was actually 81 percent name recognition in the United States, according to an April 2011 Ipsos study. The global name recognition was 79 percent, and climbed as high as 92 percent in Australia. See "Ipsos Global @dvisory: Julian Assange and WikiLeaks," Ipsos, 26 April 2011, archive.today/BnV1S

ES: That's interesting. So, on the assumption that the current legal stuff is all resolved, the next few years are . . . What happens with WikiLeaks? For us, *T* equals zero is a year from now—so we're thinking about a year from now, next year, the next year. Does WikiLeaks just become bigger, more donors, more technology? Are you going to change it in some way?

JA: There are lots of changes. I think this idea I have about how to structure intellectual information is important and we will overlay that.

ES: So that's actually a part of your plan that you're talking about?

JA: Yes. When you have such public recognition you have the luxury of being able to take fairly complex intellectual ideas and push them up—ideas that would normally take a long time to organically get traction—like Sun did with Java, for example.[257] We can put our weight behind them and push them up. But I've also seen that it's very difficult for us to be a command-and-control organization. You spoke about the difficulties that you had to learn with Novell, but for us as an organization, we are in a position where we have the full force of a superpower and its investigative organs, and the rest of NATO, operating against us, bribing people, monitoring communications, et cetera.[258] That

---

257. From 1983 until 1997, Eric Schmidt worked at Sun Microsystems, Inc., where, as chief technology officer and corporate executive officer, he led project development on the Java programming language.

258. Before he was hired by Larry Page and Sergey Brin to helm Google in 2002, Eric Schmidt was the CEO and chairman of Novell.

means that for us any little psychological weakness in our people, any friction between our people, can lead to those forces picking them off.

ES: Oh, you could be infiltrated even, in theory.

JA: Yes. The picking off is, I think, a bigger problem. But you are right about the infiltration.

ES: But the forces opposed to you, they will think, okay, this is a foreign actor, let's send our agent in, become a member, discover all their secrets.

JA: Right, and we are aware of that problem and we investigate people. But that has tremendously slowed down our growth, because we can't just put an ad out and say we want you to have these skills and come into the office; it is absolutely impossible. So our growth is constrained in that way. But there is another way of leading, and that's leading through values instead of through command and control. When you lead through values you don't need to trust people, and there is no limit on the number of people who can adopt those values and the speed at which they can adopt them. It all happens very quickly. It's not supply-limited—in terms of employees supply—rather it's demand-limited; as soon as people demand a value they adopt it.

ES: I see that. The way I express that is that the power of an idea is underappreciated. That if you can get the idea inserted correctly then millions of people buy it. My comment would be that the deeper ideas that you are talking about are either not understood or they are being fought by misinformation. As you said, it's a clever use of words, turned against you, what have you. So you have a challenge to get the deeper arguments that you have made to us heard over all these other forces.

JA: If you say lies for long enough people start to believe them. "The Afghan release was a terrible thing"—that has spread so fast that we have basically given up trying to knock it down. The energy is better spent doing something else. But we are educating a whole range of people about us and our values and the things that we believe in. What is happening is that these people are finding each other across the world and across states. We are creating our own computational network of human beings that can think in the same way, that can trust each other on a point-to-point basis. We started last year in a position where we had this big confrontation with the State Department and the Pentagon at the same time. One of our few claims to success is that we've managed to get the Pentagon and the State Department to cooperate!

[*Laughter*]

They are internally highly organized; they have their contact sheets; they have an internal mail system; they have their command-and-control structure where they can task people and pour resources into things; and they have people available to spend time on us. Maybe there are 10,000. In that particular case that is who is pushing against us. On the other hand, on our side we have millions of people around the world who support us and support our values, who are traditionally completely atomized. There is no command-and-control structure; they are not able to effectively coordinate with each other, and so on. That's the starting condition, but of course an organization starts to form as these people find each other locally. As they discover each other they become optimized—that network of nodes starts linking up and becoming more and more efficient at comprehending its environment, planning for action, and then acting. We have plans to potentiate that. We are going to take these graphs of several million supporters, and—do you know what simulated annealing is?

ES: No.

JA: When you are trying to make an alloy you have two different metals and the idea is that you put these metals together. You mix them together and the molecules of the two different metals settle into an arrangement with each other where they are in the tightest attraction to each other—the lowest energy state. To get them into this state can be quite hard, because one molecule might be buddied up with another to its left, but the strongest arrangement might be if it joins the molecules to its right, so it needs a kick to get out of the position it is in and into this new position. This is called annealing. When people are making these alloys they melt the metals together, pour them, then let them cool a bit, and then heat them up a bit, let them cool a bit, heat them up a bit; but not so much each time. They might even do things like smack them, hit them, and physically smash them. We have a system we're developing where we will put all these people into a network which we will anneal, using a simulated annealing method, so that there is the tightest possible human arrangement between these million people.

ES: Around the set of principles.

JA: Around the set of principles. That's the unifier.

ES: I see.

JA: And then we will have an efficient computational network—in terms of human computation—which can observe, plan, and act.

TOTAL PUBLISHING

ES: Another criticism, I think, with respect to WikiLeaks: you were careful, according to the reports, to work to redact sensitive information. As I understand it, there was an editing process, somebody had to build a specialized search engine because the documents were so complicated, there was a fairly lengthy review period with the mainstream media, et cetera. That's all fairly well documented. Now, imagine another person, not you, who does not have the same values but has the same technology, because the technology is obviously copyable—what happens when there is more of them than there are of you? Or one of them and one of you?

JA: Well, who holds WikiLeaks accountable? We have our values. How do people see whether we are sticking to our values or whether we have betrayed our values? Maybe people don't like our values; maybe they do. How can the human economic ecosystem discipline us or encourage us in particular directions?

Sources speak with their feet. If sources believe that we are going to protect them, and that we are going to have higher impact for the material, they will simply give us material instead of giving it to someone else. So that's one way in which we are disciplined by the market of sources.

ES: So it is a selection bias, basically.

JA: The question is, could sources pick another group that was going to publish without any harm-minimization procedure at all? The answer is yes, but one has to understand the primary reason we engage in harm-minimization procedures. It's not primarily because the material we release will have a reasonable risk of producing harm as a result of disclosure. That's very rare. Rather, there is a probable risk that if we don't engage in that sort of behavior our opponents will opportunistically attempt to distract from the revelations that we have published—very important matters—by instead speaking about whether there is a potential for harm, and therefore whether this release is hypocritical—given that we want to promote justice—and whether the organization is hypocritical. And so a lot of the procedures that we engage in are not merely to try to minimize risk to people who might be named in the material; rather, it is to minimize the risk that opportunists will reduce the impact of the material when it is released. So part of the impact-maximization that we do is to prevent this type of attack on what we publish. From that point of view intelligence sources will understand that we do it in order to maximize impact. Now that said, we do not permanently redact anything. We only do delayed redactions. So we delay until the security situation has changed and we can release the information.

ES: So is it fair to say that eventually the things that you redacted will all be made available?

JA: Yes.

LS: That's a different question, actually, from what you were asking, which was, what if the same process and technology fell into—

JA: Yes, I'm getting to that. We have all sorts of other projects about syndicating our submission system to third parties. It disturbs me that we are redacting at all. It is a very, very dangerous slippery slope. And I've already said that we go through this not merely to minimize harm but for political considerations, to stop people distracting from the important part of the material by instead hyping up concerns about risks.

JC: It's a pragmatic decision. A strategic decision.

JA: It's a pragmatic, tactical decision to keep the maximum impact there, instead of having to be distracted. But here we are already engaging in a rather dangerous compromise, although not nearly to the same degree as the newspapers do. We have collaborated with them and seen that some of them are just appalling. We released an analysis of their redactions versus what actually needed to be redacted, and it is extremely interesting.[259]

ES: So there was a difference of view on what needed to be redacted?

JA: The *Guardian* redacted two-thirds of a cable about Bulgarian crime. It removed all the names of the mafiosi who had infil-

---

259. For examples, see the cabledrum website:
www.cabledrum.net/pages/censorship.php
Both cables.mrkva.eu and cablegatesearch.net provide excellent ways of comparing redacted versions of cables with full versions, in order to see what WikiLeaks' media partners redacted.

trated the Bulgarian government.[260] It removed a description of the Kazakhstan elite, which said that the Kazakhstan elite in general was corrupt—not even a particular name, just in general. It removed a description of an Italian energy company operating in Kazakhstan as being corrupt.[261] So they have redacted individual names of people who might be unfairly put at risk, just like we do—that is what we require of them. They have redacted the names

---

260. In this example the original cable contained 5,226 words. The redacted version published by the *Guardian* had only 1,406 words. For the original cable see canonical ID: 05SOFIA1207_a, Public Library of US Diplomacy, WikiLeaks, archive.today/ryqvN

   For the *Guardian* redacted version see, "US embassy cables: Organised crime in Bulgaria," *Guardian*, 1 December 2010, archive.today/faYa6

   For the *Guardian* news story based on the cable see, "WikiLeaks cables: Russian government 'using mafia for its dirty work,'" *Guardian*, 1 December 2010, archive.today/WYKEe

   The extent of the redaction can be seen visually on the Cablegatesearch website, which shows the revision history, with the redactions shaded in pink: archive.today/rdVYl

   This Bulgarian example is discussed by WikiLeaks' Bulgarian media partner *Bivol* in, "Unedited cable from Sofia shows the total invasion of the state by organized crime (Update: Cable Comparison)," *WL Central*, 18 March 2011, archive.today/kmvLt

   In addition see, "The Guardian: Redacting, censoring or lying?" *WL Central*, 19 March 2012, archive.today/YR3VN

   Also of note below both *WL Central* stories is the comment from *Guardian* journalist David Leigh and the responses.

261. For the original cable see, canonical ID: 10ASTANA72_a, Public Library of US Diplomacy, WikiLeaks, archive.today/VSyHl

   For the *Guardian* redacted version see, "US embassy cables: Kazakhstan—the big four," *Guardian*, 29 November 2010, archive.today/O08ut

   The redaction can be seen visually on the Cablegatesearch website, which shows the revision history, with the redactions shaded in pink: archive.today/Nm1k4

of individual mafiosi, because they are worried that they might get sued for libel in London. They have redacted the description of a societal class as being corrupt. And they have redacted descriptions of individual companies being corrupt because they don't want to expose themselves to any risk at all. And that's true of the *Irish Independent*, even though it's a very good newspaper and the journalists are totally onside, they do this. It is incredible self-censorship across the board and they don't admit to doing it or reveal the fact that they are doing it. WikiLeaks does not want to go down that path. I'm sure all these institutions started out by saying, "No, we will just do these little redactions." And then economics comes into play, and then they think, "Why take the risk?" You end up with a system of self-censorship. And it is embarrassing to do it, so why tell the public that you are doing it?[262] If you are not telling the public you are doing it, it gets easier and easier to do every time.[263]

If we look at email, no one censors email. Look at a telephone call to your grandmother—is there a censor sitting there on the line determining whether you are about to say something bad to your grandmother and cutting it out? Of course not. The postal system—are there people opening envelopes to see whether you are

262. A documentary co-produced by WikiLeaks and Sixteen Films, *Mediastan* (2013), included an interview with the *Guardian* editor Alan Rusbridger in which Rusbridger goes into the reasons for the *Guardian's* self-censorship. The segment is available on YouTube. "Mediastan: The Rushbridger [*sic*] extract" (video), uploaded 11 October 2013, youtu.be/ZNgFDFibit0

263. For further discussion of this point with more specific examples, see Julian Assange with Jacob Appelbaum, Andy Müller-Maguhn, and Jérémie Zimmermann, *Cypherpunks: Freedom and the Future of the Internet* (OR Books, 2012), pp. 121–122.

sending something bad? No. YouTube—a priori, is anyone sitting there reviewing every video before it's posted?

ES: Let me give you the technical answer, to make sure you know it. We can't review every submission, so basically the crowd marks it if it's a problem.

JA: Yes, but post-publication?

ES: Post-publication.

JA: So once it is out, people could take copies and it could be spreading everywhere.

ES: And what happens is the takedown of . . . We get into trouble because various players want us to do pre-publication review. But with forty-eight hours of YouTube video coming in every minute, we can't mechanically do it. So if someone posts something wrong or evil or a violation of law, whatever, there is a gap, hopefully short, between the time that it's published and marked for further review against our policies. And the policies are well specified in a document.

JA: Yes.

LS: It's a pretty high bar, though, to take stuff down. It's not just wrong as in factually wrong.

ES: But under the way that these things work, commercial websites, we can decide what we want to allow and what we don't. We have a set of criteria; you can see them, you can read them. We want some kinds of videos and not other kinds of videos and you can't violate copyright and all that kind of stuff.

JA: I rather like what happened to Collateral Murder. Collateral Murder instantly got flagged up by our opponents as rated over eighteen, so no one could see it directly on YouTube without logging in, but as an embed they could see it just fine.[264] My interpretation of this is that when there is an embed someone else's brand is on the damn thing; and when there's not an embed Google's brand is on it![265]

[*Laughter*]

ES: Without knowing the specifics, all I can tell you is the system is responsive to the post-publication feedback. There have been a couple of cases in YouTube where there have been ratings scams where, you know, Jared will publish a document and people will decide they want to demote him. So they will give him a lot of negatives because he is being attacked and he becomes unfairly lower ranked than he really should be. So these systems are manipulable by pressure groups, and I would think that would be a constant in this case.

JC: Sometimes by regimes—there are some autocratic regimes that will flag content posted by activists as inappropriate.

JA: We've had stuff flagged that we have posted; anti-Scientologists have had the same. I think there were 5,000 Scientology videos

---

264. A YouTube video can be embedded in a website so that it can be viewed directly on that website without having to go to YouTube.

265. YouTube is owned by Google.

removed from YouTube when some lawyer swore that they were all his copyright.[266]

Because we deal with almost purely political material—I don't mean party-political, I mean how power is delegated—there is such scrutiny on us at this moment that if we were to switch to a publish-first, pull-later model they would say, "Oh, well it's too late! You've put it out there, now there are a thousand copies!"

ES: You have a different model. You require human editors.

JA: It is a severe problem, though. It means that, in terms of scalability, things are very hard for us. That's why we have this new syndication system where we are syndicating the editing to various nonprofits and so on.

ES: But you are fundamentally outsourcing the human judgment, because it's not possible today to write computer algorithms to do this for you.

JA: There is some cost to publishing without vetting, but actually the problems of vetting before publication are so severe that they are a much, much greater problem. If you have to choose between those two, you would choose publication without vetting.

ES: That's also interesting to us. That says you would fundamentally prefer . . . You are so concerned about this human judgment and the possibility of bias—

---

266. "Massive Takedown of Anti-Scientology Videos on YouTube," Electronic Frontier Foundation, 5 September 2008, archive.today/fQ1Do

[*Period of wind interference*]

JA: We'd ask the source to do it. We'd put the weight on the people giving us the material: "You exercise your judgment about what you send us, but everything you send us we are going to publish." Otherwise we will be compromised and once other people understand that we have a lever to determine what is published and what is not, they will try to get at that lever.

JC: Well, actually I have a follow-up question on that. Again, we're looking futuristically, in each aspect of the book, and what I wonder is—you have a certain volume of content that you are getting right now, at one point Twitter only had so much content as well, and at a certain point it does become so overwhelming that if you publish everything that gets sent at what point is there such a mixture, is there so much content that it's just manipulated that it essentially drowns out the legitimate—

JA: The manipulated content will never be the issue, although there is something to be said for having a perfect record, which we do at the moment. But manipulated content will always be an insignificant quantity of material. The reason is that it takes economic work to manipulate content. To do it well you need someone who is even more intelligent than the person who created the original document, even more informed. And if the whole document is going public this is not like a news story where you only give the journalist manipulated content. You have to fool all your opponents and everyone else in the world with the material; it's a lot harder. At the same time, every organization generates a mountain of paperwork and internal records just by virtue of its activities, so all of those records are produced for free. The legitimate content will always outweigh the manipulated content. The problem is that a small amount of manipulated content can devalue the large amount of unmanipulated content.

ES: Can I disagree with you on one point? I fundamentally believe that disinformation becomes so easy to generate, because complexity overwhelms knowledge, that it's in people's interest, if you will, over the next decade, to build disinformation-generating systems. This is true for corporations, for marketing, for governments, and so forth. And it makes the job for a legitimate journalist that much harder, right? And your answer earlier was that this is fundamentally a trust problem, which I think is roughly correct. I would argue that it's fundamentally a ranking problem. Ranking is based on trust and other algorithms; it's the same conclusion. But it's not, in my view, correct to say that there will always be more factually correct information than a small amount of manipulated information. It is perfectly reasonable that the actors will see that computer AI systems can generate a lot of false stuff.[267] You're well aware of the projects to write papers by computer.

JA: Yes, I've seen those. Everyone always thought that we would get flooded with those, and it never happened. If you exclude the nutters going on about how at a garden party one night twelve years ago, speaking to his ex-wife with a pot plant in between them, she told him that he was the Antichrist, and he understood it was true . . .

[Laughter]

---

267. "AI" stands for "artificial intelligence."

If you exclude those cases, which we get a fair bit of, there have been about twenty genuine attempted frauds. It's extraordinary, it's almost nothing.

ES: No, but you could make the argument that that's a statement about altruism and good, and that the steps required to actually manipulate are hard enough that you have to be pretty badly intended. The threshold for doing that is pretty high.

JA: So what is the closest? It's the pump-and-dump scams in stocks, for instance.[268] That's the one that we see fairly frequently, and where they've done it as GIFs and they even have things to evade OCR recognition on emails.[269]

ES: In Google's case we see lots and lots of link farms which are attempting to manipulate our rankings. And we detect them.

---

268. A "pump-and-dump" scam is a classic stock market scam where the scammer buys shares of stock with low liquidity and then "pumps" the stock— creates rumors that it is about to go up. If successful, many people buy the stock, and the price is driven up, at which point the scammer "dumps" his shares—selling them all at the inflated price before the price crashes back to normal.

269. "OCR" stands for "optical character recognition," a way to translate images of text (such as from scans) to characters that the computer can recognize.

The advent of email, and with it, email spam, provided new ways for scammers to "pump." In order to get around spam filters that look out for stock-related keywords, scammers took to sending their spam as GIF image files, which were designed to be unreadable for machines using the OCR technology but still readable for their intended human victims.

JA: HBGary, a high-tech intelligence contractor, was asked by Bank of America to submit a tender to take us down.[270] We got hold of their copy of the tender. We don't know who ended up taking the tender. The quote was $2 million a month, for which they would spread disinformation, hack, target our journalists; they would have network maps of people who supported us and they would leverage their careers and self-interests against their ideology. So that's there, but disinformation has always been there. I'm not sure why it should increase relative to the information increase we are seeing everywhere else.

ES: This, by the way, is a fundamental argument against something you and I talked about earlier. We do actually need to resolve this.

SM: Arm wrestling maybe?

[*Laughter*]

JC: This is actually one of the most interesting . . . The whole conversation has been fascinating but this last piece is really fascinating because it plays into how Eric and I and Scott are thinking about these chapters. It's like, imagine ten years from now, or imagine fifteen years. So for the purposes of argument, let's imagine, ten years from now it's very easy not just for a large group of people to create fake documents, produce them en masse, and distribute them en masse. Let's assume a single individual has that capacity through the technological platforms they have at their disposal.

---

270. For more on the HBGary incident, see "Background on US v. WikiLeaks," page 205.

JA: You won't have Julian Assange saying it's true, or whoever.

ES: [Julian] is making a more fundamental argument. He's saying that humankind does not organize itself that way. There are enough barriers that the moral choice, if you will, of me acting to do all of that, tends to limit the amount of it, because otherwise there would have already been a lot of it.

JC: So let's assume a government then, which would have the motivation to potentially do something.

JA: They do all that now. The strategic communications propaganda arm of the Pentagon costs something like $6 billion a year.[271]

SM: But has anyone done it through you? In other words, government versus government using WikiLeaks as a laundry.

JA: We don't care as long as it's true. If it's true information we don't care where it comes from. Let people fight with the truth, and when the bodies are cleared there will be bullets of truth everywhere, that's fine.

SM: But that does take your editorial capacity just back to verification.

---

271. An Associated Press investigation found that between 2004 and 2009 the money the US military spent on "winning hearts and minds" grew by 63 percent to $4.7 billion. The Department of Defense's public relations, advertising, and recruitment staff, at 27,000 employees, was by that time almost as large as the entire State Department workforce. That year, one project alone attempted to launder over 10,000 public relations influencers into the media, including 5,400 press releases, 3,000 television releases, and 1,600 interviews. See "Pentagon Spending Billions on PR to Sway World Opinion," Fox News, 5 February 2009, archive.today/30Npv

JC: Right, because it's different than just saying we'll publish everything.

SM: It's a different slippery slope but it's still a slippery slope.

JA: No, I think it's not at all. I think that is the whole intent: let people fight with the truth.

ES: But the argument is that there has to be a choice algorithm, you have to have some way of knowing that you're dealing with a legitimate source and the source can choose the publisher.

SM: No, I understand that but that's why the ecology is biased against any society where you can't verify. Then those people are left on their own. WikiLeaks can't help them. WikiLeaks just says, "When you get a good verification system, then we're good. Otherwise, good luck, whatever."

LS: But they're verifying documents, they're not verifying facts.

JC: No, they are verifying sources.

JA: No, no, we don't verify sources; we verify that documents are official documents.

LS: Right, they are official documents.

SM: You do in part have to be verifying the sources, though.

LS: But it's also not verifying facts, and so it's not about truth.

JA: It's not about verifying facts, yeah.

SM: Well, that's another argument. Ha-ha-ha. It's about verifying documents; not verifying truth!

JC: This takes us back to the noise argument, right? It's not just in a context of revolution that technology generates noise. They're going to be faced with more noise in the future and the question isn't whether human beings prefer truth over fiction but whether or not they can find the truth and tell it from the fiction.

ES: But that's the core question. He disagrees with me on this point. We have to resolve this.

JA: We have published all the fake documents that we have received that were interesting. We published saying that they were fake.

JC: Like, WikiForgeries?

JA: But there's not that many to bother with. But actually, they are not fake; on a meta level they are true forgeries.

ES: They are very interesting in and of themselves, right?

JA: Very interesting in and of themselves. One was an attempt to influence the Kenyan election by saying that the opposition had signed a secret agreement with the Islamic minority to introduce Sharia law across Kenya.[272] It sounds ridiculous, but actually it was carefully constructed.

JC: So how do you know if they are forgeries?

---

272. "MOU between Raila Odinga and Muslims," WikiLeaks, 14 November 2007, archive.today/giXkU

JA: Well, that one was hard—that was a carefully constructed document. We checked signatures and we found the real one. That was hard work. Usually it's not hard work.

JC: But it requires human capital to do, right?

JA: Yes. Usually someone makes an elementary mistake. There is a disincentive to sending us a forgery because we are perceived as being quite good at detecting them and we make the whole document public. So why wouldn't you just give it to a newspaper, because they don't make the document public, and the newspaper doesn't have expertise in that domain? It's a lot easier to overcome them.

This bigger issue you're talking about, let's say you don't have authenticators like us. Authentication is hard. We can't authenticate the amount of material we are getting in. So we have thought about ways to deal with this, of having a great big mesh of people with information flowing through it and different people adding their authentications as it flows through. It would distribute and delegate that task. That might pan out.

But what if everyone was simply publishing anonymously, and you had no authenticators? What would happen? To begin with, you would just have a completely flat structure. Let's say information there is all just addressed by a hash or something. So there's no structure at all, there's just this document and that document and that document and so on. Then you will have people who want influence making robots that put a whole load of garbage everywhere. But it's not tied in to any structure. So how does anyone get to anything? Do they hear it from their friends and then go and look at it? Do they link it into their webpages?

ES: It creates an influence graph of some kind.

JA: Yes, there is some kind of influence graph that you use to get to information. You can flood the internet with information—that doesn't mean you're going to flood the influence graph with information. That's something that's different.

ES: But that's the modern story of ranking. The web is full of spam, but spam gets ranked low because of influence and the link structure and so forth. I think we should see if we can finish up, as the sun is coming on out.

THE PROCESS IS THE END GAME

JC: As we're walking can I ask you one last question that I was wondering along the way? Scott talked about the subculture that's developed around all this, which is a really interesting idea for us to explore in the book because it raises this question of, does the subculture create the demand that leads to the creation of the technology or does the technology in fact create the subculture? It's an interesting cause-and-effect argument.

JA: Well, you can argue this on both sides, but I think the technology permits the subculture. Once you have a whole bunch of young people who can communicate their ideas and values freely, then culture arises naturally. That culture comes out of experiences and harmonizing with other cultures and stuff already in the record, but it also just comes out of the temperament of young people—the desire to find allies and friends and share in a process and to remove power from old people!

LS: Ha-ha-ha-ha-ha.

SM: It's remarkable how uncreative old people are.

ES: Speaking as an older person, I agree.

SM: I speak as one as well.

ES: I think part of your intellectual argument is that in the model you are using, the Stanford model, you start off with human values, and then they get co-opted if you will, my word not yours, with the status model—you are forced into the structure.[273] The incentive system and constraints put you into this box as you get older.

JA: Right, exactly. And with different systems that potentiate different ways of transmitting wealth or communicating values or making some types of group cognition more efficient than others.

ES: Right. And your argument is that if you get enough of this new group that you identify together, it is in fact a summary change in these complex systems.

JA: Right. It will be interesting to see whether we have some sort of state change as well. A revolution is a big state change; everything was in one state and then it collapses into another state. And those transitions happen very quickly. It will be interesting to see whether we will have a broader, general, globalized cultural change that has this fast transition. It's possible.

ES: Yeah. One thing I have learned is that things happen fast because of globalization because everything is interconnected. It didn't used to be true.

---

273. This is a reference back to the discussion about the culture at Stanford University in 1971.

JA: Information, money, and wealth. The big issue with globalization is that you can be an asshole and move your money elsewhere. Fast EFTs, fast wealth movements, fast signing of contracts (which are a type of wealth movement)—these encourage opportunism.[274] Because if money can move faster than political sanction, you can just keep moving the money through the system, and growing it as it moves through the system, and having it become more and more powerful, and by the time the moral outrage comes to stop it, it's too late, it has gone. So what's happening now on the internet is that political sanction . . . I use "political" the way Australians use it, by the way, which is not about party politics.

SM: Oh, is that Australian?

ES: The body politic.

JA: Yes, the body politic. Political sanction is now able to move a lot faster than it did before—possibly as fast as money. Not in any individual transfer, but in the complex structuring arrangements you need to make transfers, these can take a while.

SM: Are you going to think of another question, Eric? You're beginning to get like Columbo. Julian, you've been so generous with your time.

JC: Really appreciate it.

LS: Do you have a bracelet?

---

274. "EFT" stands for "electronic funds transfer."

JA: I do, on my leg—a manacle.

LS: A manacle!

ES: And, just out of curiosity, as you get ready for the next court thing you have to go through, unfortunately, the legal team comes over and visits every day?

JA: Well, they can't come out here every day from London. It's eight hours' traveling per day. Actually I just fired part of my old legal team.

ES: Yeah, I just saw that. Do you end up on the phone a lot?

JA: They were charging, after promising not to, 730 pounds an hour to sit on a train coming out from London.

ES: I see.

JA: I am rather unhappy about it.

ES: But at the end of the day do you end up having visitors every day, basically? Or is this relatively unusual?

JA: My staff and so on.

ES: Yeah.

JA: More interesting visitors every week or so.

ES: Well, I hope we have been at least a distraction!

[*Laughter*]

JA: We wouldn't mind a leak from Google, which would be, I think, probably all the Patriot Act requests.[275]

ES: Which would be [*whispers*] illegal.

[*Nervous chuckles*]

JA: It depends on the jurisdiction . . . !

[*Chuckles*]

ES: We are a US—

JA: There are higher laws. First Amendment, you know.

ES: No, I've actually spent quite a bit of time on this question because I am in great trouble because I have given a series of criticisms about Patriot I and Patriot II, because they're nontransparent, because the judge's orders are hidden and so forth and so on. The answer is that the laws are quite clear about Google in the US. We couldn't do it. It would be illegal.

JA: We're fighting this case now, with Twitter. We've done three court hearings trying to get the names of the other companies that fulfilled the subpoenas for the grand jury in the US. Twitter resisted the subpoena and that's how some of us became aware.[276] They argued that we should be told that there was a subpoena. I wasn't told but three other people were told.

---

275. For context on this, see "Background on US v. WikiLeaks," page 205.

276. For more on the "Twitter subpoena case" see "Background on US v. WikiLeaks," page 205.

SM: And this was concerning you, concerning WikiLeaks?

JA: Yes, me personally. But we know there are at least four other companies.

ES: I can certainly pass on your request to our general counsel.

JA: Tell them to argue that we should be told.

ES: So your specific request is that Google argue legally—

JA: Yes.

ES: —that WikiLeaks as an organization should be informed—

JA: Or any of the individuals.

ES: —or the individuals, if they are named in a FISA.[277]

JA: Yes.

ES: Okay. I will pass that along.[278]

JA: Great.

---

277. In this specific instance "a FISA" is shorthand for "a FISA request," in other words a legal request for electronic records pursuant to FISA. "FISA" stands for "Foreign Intelligence Surveillance Act," a United States law that authorizes electronic and physical surveillance, now infamous throughout the world after the Snowden leaks about how FISA and the FISA court operate. For the best overview of FISA, see "Surveillance Under the Foreign Intelligence Surveillance Act (FISA)," Electronic Frontier Foundation, archive.today/ibU4C

278. For context on this, see "Background on US v. WikiLeaks," page 205.

ES: And we'll see what comes back!

JA: Tell them to bring back all the other's ones as well.

[*Laughter*]

ES: Why don't we all figure out what we are going to do next in a minute, but let's let Julian get back to actually running the empire. The other thing is, in terms of running WikiLeaks—I keep asking questions—I'm just curious, running WikiLeaks, are you able? You have a staff so you have to talk to them.

JA: Yes.

ES: Call them? I assume you can do email and all that, no?

JA: I don't use email.

ES: Because it's bugged?

JA: It's too dangerous. And encrypted email is possibly even worse, because it's such a flag for end-point attacks. It's like, attack that end point, attack that end point, that's an encrypted email. But we do have encrypting phones. Unfortunately they don't work in all countries, but the SMSs work in all countries.

ES: When you speak with a staff member, would it typically be on the phone or in person?

JA: Typically in person. I have to act like Osama Bin Laden now.

JC: How big is the staff, Julian?

JA: About twenty.

ES: But roughly, then, if I were to describe it, people come and visit, you're using technology carefully to manage things, and you're well aware of people watching you, and so forth.

JA: Yes.

ES: And that's been true for a while, I think, from reading about it.

JA: That's been true for at least a year and a . . . One of our early cryptographers was ambushed by British intelligence in a Luxembourg car park in early 2008, that was the first concrete—

ES: What did they do?

JA: They followed him there to a supermarket, and when he came out of the supermarket they were waiting by the car. A man in his forties, nice watch, good shoes, confident, tall, British accent—a James Bond. Very stereotyped character. He started to ask questions about WikiLeaks and me, and told him it would be in his interest to come and have a cup of coffee and have a chat about things. But it was a clear threat—it was a supermarket car park. He could have made that approach somewhere else. It was made in the car park of a supermarket.

LS: Did he self-identify as British intelligence?

JA: No. Our guy left, saying he wasn't interested in men.

[Laughter]

LS: How do you know if you've won?

JA: If I've won? If we've won?

JC: Lisa asked the best question of the day.

ES: How do you know if you've won?

JA: It's not possible to win this kind of thing. This is a continuous striving that people have been doing for a long time. Of course, there are many individual battles that we win, but it is the nature of human beings that they lie and cheat and deceive. Organized groups of people who do not lie and cheat and deceive find each other and get together. Because they have that temperament, they are more efficient, because they are not lying and cheating and deceiving each other. That is a very old struggle between opportunists and collaborators. I don't see that going away. I think we can make some significant advances and perhaps it is the making of these advances and being involved in that struggle that is good for people. The process is part of the end game. It's not just to get somewhere in the end; rather, this process of people feeling that it is worthwhile to be involved in that sort of struggle, is in fact worthwhile for people.

SM: That's a satisfyingly spiritual ending.

[*Laughter*]

LS: How do we get the beginning part of what you have on tape to transcribe, how would you like us to do that?

JA: I might give it to you now; it might be safest.

LS: If you don't mind? And then we'll transcribe it and send it all back to you? Could we just FedEx it?

JA: Yes.

LS: Is that . . . safe?

[*End of tape*]

DELIVER US FROM "DON'T BE EVIL"

Readers might be interested to know how WikiLeaks and the causes it stands for were eventually represented in *The New Digital Age*, to compare against the source material.

In bringing up WikiLeaks—a taboo of sorts in US State Department circles—Schmidt and Cohen feel the need to apologize. "Our . . . position aside," they explain, "we must account for what free-information activists may try to do in the future, and therefore, Assange is a useful starting point." Their own view is that "greater transparency in all things [to] bring about a more just, safe and free world" is "a dangerous model": "governments have systems and valuable regulations in place that, while imperfect, should continue to govern who gets to make the decision about what is classified and what is not."[279]

With their audience suitably reassured, they go on to offer a polite and high-minded summary. They relate my observation that human civilization is built on our intellectual record, obliging us to make that record as large as possible, searchable, and resistant to censorship. They describe one of the theoretical underpinnings of

---

279. Eric Schmidt and Jared Cohen, *The New Digital Age*, British paperback edition (John Murray, 2013), pp. 39–40.

WikiLeaks—that the release of leaked information can only harm organizations that are engaged in acts which the public does not support, and that such organizations cannot help but to produce this incriminating material if they wish to remain efficient. And they explain my concerns about censorship through complexity, where extremely complicated arrangements, such as those seen in the offshore financial sector, are ostensibly open but completely impenetrable.

Summary done, the authors proceed to use WikiLeaks to position themselves. They briskly conclude that it is "unfortunate" that "people like Assange and organizations like WikiLeaks will be well placed to take advantage of some of the changes in the next decade."[280]

Why do they think it is unfortunate? Schmidt and Cohen fall back on a discredited 2010 Pentagon talking point: "The information released on WikiLeaks put lives at risk."[281] No evidence is given in the text—and unqualified references to risk are intellectually void anyhow—but there is a footnote. Unfortunately, anyone hoping to find even the source of this accusation will be disappointed. "At a minimum," the note states, "platforms like WikiLeaks and hacker collectives that traffic in stolen classified material from governments enable or encourage espionage."[282]

Espionage is, of course, different from putting "lives at risk"— one loose accusation has been backed up by adding another—but no evidence is offered that WikiLeaks "enables" espionage either.

---

280. Ibid., p. 41.

281. Ibid., p. 163.

282. Ibid., note 3, Chapter 5, p. 163.

Although it is incoherent to equate publishing with the private sale of secrets to states, Schmidt and Cohen do just that.

Invoking espionage is no light matter. Chelsea Manning is serving a thirty-five-year prison sentence after being convicted with creatively applied espionage charges. A key aim of the prosecution in her trial was to embroil me in those same espionage charges, at once criminalizing both whistleblowing and publishing.

Schmidt and Cohen ask their readers, "Why is it Julian Assange, specifically, who gets to decide what information is relevant to the public interest?" and "what happens if the person who makes such decisions is willing to accept indisputable harm to innocents as a consequence of his disclosures?"[283] But the authors' imputations of "harm" are at odds even with the US government. Brigadier General Robert Carr, a US counterintelligence official, was forced to admit during the Manning trial, under oath, that despite a thorough and presumably politically desperate search, no instances could be found of an individual being physically harmed as a result of WikiLeaks' releases.[284] A senior NATO official in Kabul told CNN in October 2010 that "there has not been a single case of Afghans needing protection or to be moved because of the leak."[285]

If Schmidt and Cohen do not think "Julian Assange, specifically" should decide what information is relevant to the public, who should? In most societies such judgments are the job of

283. Ibid., p. 42.

284. Ed Pilkington, "Bradley Manning leak did not result in deaths by enemy forces, court hears," *Guardian*, 31 July 2013, archive.today/lYznz

285. Adam Levine, "Gates: Leaked documents don't reveal key intel, but risks remain," CNN, 17 October 2010, archive.today/HzJxM

publishers and journalists independent, as they are supposed to be, of government. Perhaps Schmidt and Cohen do believe in journalism, but "specifically" not in journalism published by WikiLeaks. Alas, no.

The institution they have in mind to determine who should publish what is the state.

Whistleblowing publishers, they tell us, need "supervision" in order to serve a positive role in society. As for who should conduct this supervision, they suggest "a central body facilitating the release of information."[286] No more detail is offered, and none of the obvious dangers of this totalitarian vision are discussed.

Writing before the emergence of Edward Snowden, Schmidt and Cohen speculate that future leaks are less likely because governments and corporations are "now wise to the risks that lackluster cybersecurity allows."[287] They ask themselves whether WikiLeaks-like uncensorable publishers will proliferate—a "compelling and frightening idea"—and decide that in the West they will not, but some developing countries will "experience their own version of the WikiLeaks phenomenon" as they come online.[288]

"Organizations that cannot consistently attract high-level leaks will lose attention and funding, slowly but surely atrophying in the process," the authors explain. "Assange described this dynamic from his organization's perspective as a positive one, providing a check on

---

286. Eric Schmidt and Jared Cohen, *The New Digital Age*, British paperback edition (John Murray, 2013), p. 42.

287. Ibid., p. 44.

288. Ibid., p. 42, p. 44.

WikiLeaks as surely as it kept them in business. 'Sources speak with their feet,' he said. 'We're disciplined by market forces.'"[289]

I actually said, "We are disciplined by the market of sources"—an insignificant error. But a serious slur follows it:

> Assange told us he redacted only to reduce the international pressure that was financially strangling him and said he would have preferred no redactions.[290]

This is false, but it soon found its way into various publications, such as *Foreign Policy* magazine, in pre-release publicity for Schmidt and Cohen's book, under the helpful headline "Money is the only reason Julian Assange redacted WikiLeaks files."[291]

Here is the relevant section of the transcript:

> Julian Assange: The question is, could sources pick another group that was going to publish without any harm-minimization procedure at all? The answer is yes, but one has to understand the primary reason we engage in harm-minimization procedures. It's not primarily because the material we release will have a reasonable risk of producing harm as a result of disclosure. That's very rare. Rather, there is a probable risk that if we don't engage in that sort of behavior our opponents will opportunistically attempt

---

289. Ibid., p. 45.

290. Ibid., p. 47.

291. John Hudson, "Eric Schmidt: Money is the only reason Julian Assange redacted WikiLeaks files," *Foreign Policy*, 19 April 2013, archive.today/UGU5E

to distract from the revelations that we have published—very important matters—by instead speaking about whether there is a potential for harm, and therefore whether this release is hypocritical—given that we want to promote justice—and whether the organization is hypocritical. And so a lot of the procedures that we engage in are not merely to try to minimize risk to people who might be named in the material; rather, it is to minimize the risk that opportunists will reduce the impact of the material when it is released. So part of the impact maximization that we do is to prevent this type of attack on what we publish. From that point of view intelligence sources will understand that we do it in order to maximize impact. Now that said, we do not permanently redact anything. We only do delayed redactions. So we delay until the security situation has changed and we can release the information.

Eric Schmidt: So is it fair to say that eventually the things that you redacted will all be made available?

Julian Assange: Yes. [. . .] It disturbs me that we are redacting at all. It is a very, very dangerous slippery slope. And I've already said that we go through this not merely to minimize harm but for political considerations, to stop people distracting from the important part of the material by instead hyping up concerns about risks.

There is no basis here for the assertion that I only redacted information to reduce financial and international pressure on WikiLeaks or me.

Schmidt and Cohen go on to ask themselves, "How different would the reaction have been, from Western governments in particular, if WikiLeaks had published stolen classified documents from the regimes in Venezuela, North Korea and Iran?" An answer follows:

> Taking into account the precedent President Obama set in his first term in office—a clear 'zero tolerance' approach toward unauthorized leaks of classified information from US officials—we would expect that future Western governments would ultimately adopt a dissonant posture toward digital disclosures, encouraging them abroad in adversarial countries, but prosecuting them ferociously at home."[292]

The authors later offer a practical demonstration of this kind of double standard. Although Schmidt and Cohen say that WikiLeaks is "a dangerous model" that "puts lives at risk" and "enables or encourages espionage," they willingly rely on documents released by WikiLeaks to show that China is using infrastructure projects to "extend its footprint into Africa" and its "online influence."[293]

They return to WikiLeaks in a surreal chapter called "The Future of Terrorism," under the subtitle "The Rise of Terrorist Hackers." Without historical examples of any "terrorist" hackers to refer to, they

---

292. Eric Schmidt and Jared Cohen, *The New Digital Age*, British paperback edition (John Murray, 2013), p. 47.

293. Ibid., note 111, in reference to p. 110. "Chinese telecom was contacted: WikiLeaks cable, 'Subject: stifled potential: fiber-optic cable lands in Tanzania, Origin: Embassy Dar Es Salaam (Tanzania), Cable time: Fri. 4 Sep 2009 04:48 UTC,' http://www.cablegatesearch.net/cable.php?id=09DARESSALAAM585"

fall back on "WikiLeaks . . . and its sympathetic hacker allies" as "an illustrative example." They refer to the denial-of-service protests carried out by Anonymous during "Operation Avenge Assange," which were responses to the extralegal banking blockade of WikiLeaks. It is unmentioned by the authors, but the protest took place while I was imprisoned without charge in late 2010. Three and a half years have passed, but the prosecution of the young men and women allegedly involved, the "PayPal 14," continues.[294]

The authors then insinuate that politically motivated direct action on the internet lies on the terrorism spectrum. While Schmidt and Cohen say that neither WikiLeaks nor Anonymous are terrorist groups *per se*, "some might claim that hackers who engage in activities like stealing and publishing personal and classified information online might as well be." The lines between "harmless hackers and the dangerous ones have become increasingly blurred in the post-9/11 era," they insist, busily blurring those same lines.[295]

The discussion then segues from WikiLeaks and Anonymous into more speculative avenues of moral panic, where it becomes clear that Schmidt and Cohen are out to lunch:

Whereas today we hear of middle-class Muslims living in Europe going to Afghanistan for terror-camp training, we may see the reverse in the future. Afghans and Pakistanis will go

---

294. They are being prosecuted under the same law that led to the death of internet activist Aaron Swartz, the Computer Fraud and Abuse Act, or CFAA.

295. Eric Schmidt and Jared Cohen, *The New Digital Age*, British paperback edition (John Murray, 2013), p. 163.

to Europe to learn how to be cyber terrorists. Unlike training camps with rifle ranges, monkey bars and obstacle courses, engineering boot camps could be as nondescript as a few rooms with some laptops, run by a set of technically skilled disaffected graduate students in London or Paris. Terrorist training camps today can often be identified by satellite; cyber boot camps would be indistinguishable from Internet cafes.[296]

THE NEW DIGITAL AGE AFTER SNOWDEN

In an "Afterword for the Paperback Edition," published after Edward Snowden's first disclosures, Schmidt and Cohen return to the question of leaks, but they have now abandoned the idea that future leaks are less likely. They say "there will always be too many people with access to too much information to stop bulk leaking . . . there are going to be more Assanges and Snowdens in the future."[297]

Ever occidental optimists, the authors say the outcome of the debate over Snowden's revelations will be good for the West: "We believe that ultimately it will show that in Western states with a history of protecting privacy rights, citizens and government leaders will over time effectively fine-tune the balance between liberty and security." Those living in the US are luckier still, because "even as surveillance tools become more sophisticated, the United States, with its history of calibrating the balance between ensuring public safety and preserving privacy . . . is well suited to properly re-calibrate that balance." Despite all the evidence of

---

296. Ibid., p. 165.

297. Ibid., "Afterword for the Paperback Edition."

the biggest surveillance system in the history of mankind having been constructed in the United States, Schmidt and Cohen are still stuck in a binary understanding of good states—"where both business and government leaders operate within a culture of accountability, transparency, and choice"—and bad ones, like China.

What of the responsibility of tech companies themselves? Schmidt and Cohen refer to my book review for the suggestion that they "don't appreciate how much large technology firms can threaten the liberty of individuals," but state that this "distracts us from the real question."[298] They name check Edward Snowden for insisting that technology firms "have an 'ethical obligation' to speak out more about the requests that they are receiving," but remark, "We don't think these are great arguments." Why not? The authors do not say, other than to observe that "all of us—citizens, firms, and the government—[are] still finding our way," which actually implies even greater responsibility. The authors prefer to move on to a profound lesson they draw for the US government, which is that it "needs a seat for computer scientists in the White House Situation Room." Which internet behemoth would get to place its experts around the President is not discussed.

The reality is, if, in Schmidt and Cohen's optimistic scenario, there is to be a "re-calibration" of the balance between liberty and security, it will only come about because of the bravery of Mr. Snowden and his "accomplices."[299] It is odd, then, that the authors slam Snowden for not

---

298. See "The Banality of 'Don't Be Evil,'" page 53.

299. "Accomplices" is how General James Clapper, the US Director of National Intelligence, referred to those who had assisted Edward Snowden. See DS Wright, "General Clapper Labels Journalists Snowden's 'Accomplices,'" *FireDogLake*, 30 January 2014, archive.today/91i07

acting "more responsibly" over "disclosures that may threaten national security," and are keen to highlight the "irony" that he found himself in Russia.[300] But they seem confused, because at the same time they profess to be glad that "the conversation that we've had as a country about surveillance since then has been much more robust."[301]

Reading this, it is easy to forget that Google received money from the NSA for its role in the PRISM spying program.[302] If the chairman of Google wanted a robust debate to be sparked "more responsibly," we may ask why he did not start it himself in some way, when, on a summer's day in 2011, I asked him to supply proof of what was happening. Now there's a Google Idea.

---

300. Rather than, say, highlighting the "irony" that the United States is not a safe place to exercise US First Amendment free speech rights, or the "irony" that the European Union has been so compromised by its geo-political relationship with the United States that no nation in Europe other than Russia accepted Edward Snowden's asylum requests.

301. "Afterword for the Paperback Edition" in Eric Schmidt and Jared Cohen, *The New Digital Age*, British paperback edition (John Murray, 2013).

302. Ewen MacAskill, "NSA paid millions to cover Prism compliance costs for tech companies," *Guardian*, 23 August 2013, archive.today/wNBZE

BACKGROUND ON U.S. V. WIKILEAKS

At several points in this book references are made to recent events in the story of WikiLeaks and its publishing efforts. These may be obscure to readers unfamiliar with the story of WikiLeaks, so they are summarized here.

It is WikiLeaks' mission to receive information from whistle-blowers and censored journalists, release it to the public, and then defend against the inevitable legal and political attacks. It is a routine occurrence for powerful states and organizations to attempt to suppress WikiLeaks publications, and as the publisher of last resort this is one of the hardships WikiLeaks was built to endure.

In 2010 WikiLeaks engaged in its most famous publications to date, revealing systematic abuse of official secrecy within the US military and government. These publications are known as Collateral Murder, the War Logs, and Cablegate, and were ongoing at the time of the discussion with Eric Schmidt.[303] The response has been a concerted and ongoing effort to destroy WikiLeaks by the US government and its allies.

---

303. Collateral Murder: www.collateralmurder.com
     The Iraq War Logs: www.wikileaks.org/irq
     The Afghan War Diary: www.wikileaks.org/afg
     Cablegate: www.wikileaks.org/cablegate.html

THE WIKILEAKS GRAND JURY

As a direct consequence of WikiLeaks' publications, the US government launched a multi-agency criminal investigation into Julian Assange and WikiLeaks staff, supporters, and alleged associates.

A grand jury was convened in Alexandria, Virginia, with the support of the Department of Justice and the FBI, to look into the possibility of bringing charges—including conspiracy charges under the Espionage Act of 1917—against Julian Assange and others. In grand jury proceedings no judge or defense counsel is present. US officials have said that the investigation is of "unprecedented scale and nature."

Congressional committee hearings have since heard the suggestion from members of the US Congress that the Espionage Act could be used as a tool to target journalists who "knowingly publish leaked information," suggesting that the approach is being normalized in the US justice system.[304]

WikiLeaks staff and associates were subject to covert monitoring in Germany, and later in Iceland.[305] In September 2010, while Julian Assange was traveling from Stockholm to Berlin, three encrypted WikiLeaks laptops containing privileged journalistic materials, including evidence of a war crime, disappeared while under the control of airport authorities. In 2013, WikiLeaks filed a criminal

---

304. "Congressional committee holds hearing on national security leak prevention and punishment," Reporters Committee for Freedom of the Press, 11 July 2012, archive.today/NAHgG

305. Affidavit of Julian Paul Assange, WikiLeaks, 2 September 2013, archive.today/doiGA#3

complaint with the Swedish and German authorities in connection with this incident.[306]

In August 2011, six FBI agents and two US Department of Justice prosecutors flew by private jet to Iceland and began to conduct covert interrogations in connection with the investigation into WikiLeaks, without informing the Icelandic government. Upon discovering the activities, the Icelandic government expelled the US agents.[307] They took with them an Icelandic teenager—Sigurdur Thordarson, whom they continued to interrogate in Denmark—and bribed him to turn over hard drives in his possession that contained data stolen from WikiLeaks.[308] A 2013 parliamentary investigation in Iceland uncovered that Thordarson had been turned FBI informant against WikiLeaks, and had been sent to spy on Julian Assange and WikiLeaks staff for the US investigation.[309]

In 2011 a US Air Force analyst stationed in the United Kingdom came under an internal investigation for showing signs of supporting the general mission of WikiLeaks, and attending Julian Assange's trial hearings in London. The documents from the investigation,

306. Affidavit of Julian Paul Assange, WikiLeaks, 2 September 2013, archive.today/0gUpy#5

307. Raphael Satter, "Minister: Iceland refused to help FBI on WikiLeaks," Associated Press, 1 February 2013, archive.today/Fgtyw

308. Peter Stanners, "FBI met WikiLeaks informant in Copenhagen," Copenhagen Post, 15 August 2013, archive.today/b2bL0

309. "Iceland Minister: FBI Used Hacker to Bait WikiLeaks," Iceland Review, 14 February 2013, updated 30 January 2014, archive.today/ZXsvF

released in response to a Freedom of Information request, listed "Communicating with the enemy" under "Matters alleged."[310]

In April 2014 the Department of Justice filed a court statement saying that the "multi subject" criminal investigation against WikiLeaks was "ongoing" and must continue to be kept secret.[311] Several people have been legally compelled to give evidence at grand jury hearings.[312] Associates and alleged associates of WikiLeaks have been detained at airports, deprived of their rights, and interrogated by US agents.[313] Court proceedings in the trial of Chelsea Manning,

---

310. "US Military refers to Julian Assange and WikiLeaks as the 'enemy' with the 'victims' being 'society,'" WikiLeaks, 26 September 2012, updated 27 September 2012, archive.today/vOZv5

311. "Judge in WikiLeaks FOIA Cites 'Events that Have Transpired,' Government Claims FOIA Is 'Improper,'" *emptywheel*, 10 April 2014, archive.today/QVpR7

    This was reconfirmed in May 2014. See Philip Dorling, "Assange targeted by FBI probe, US court documents reveal," *Sydney Morning Herald*, 20 May 2014, archive.today/zFhv7

    For the court documents mentioned in the *Sydney Morning Herald* story, see Case 1:12-cv-00127-BJR in the United States District Court for the District of Columbia: is.gd/hvvmgM

312. Glenn Greenwald, "WikiLeaks Grand Jury investigation widens," *Salon*, 9 June 2011, archive.today/SH0O9

313. "Part 2: Daniel Ellsberg and Jacob Appelbaum on the NDAA, WikiLeaks and Unconstitutional Surveillance," *Democracy Now!*, 6 February 2013, archive.today/gHd46

    See also Elinor Mills, "Researcher detained at U.S. border, questioned about WikiLeaks," *CNET*, 1 August 2010, archive.today/iCiPL

    See also Xeni Jardin, "WikiLeaks volunteer detained and searched (again) by US agents," *Boing Boing*, 12 January 2011, archive.today/1LtnW

    See also Paul Fontaine, "Jacob Appelbaum Detained At Keflavík Airport," *Reykjavík Grapevine*, 27 October 2011, archive.today/4AJlF

the soldier convicted of passing information to WikiLeaks, reveal an FBI file on the investigation of WikiLeaks that ran, at the time, to over 42,100 pages, some 8,000 of which referred to Manning.[314]

THE PERSECUTION OF CHELSEA MANNING

Chelsea Manning was detained without trial for 1,103 days, an infringement of her right to speedy justice. The United Nations special rapporteur for torture, Juan Mendez, formally found that Manning had been treated in a manner that was cruel and inhuman, and that possibly amounted to torture.[315] The government charged Manning—accused of being a journalistic source for WikiLeaks—with thirty-four individual counts of violations of the Uniform Code of Military Justice, including parts of the Espionage Act, the combined maximum sentence for which was over one hundred years in prison.[316]

Manning was prohibited by the court from making defense arguments as to public interest, motive, or the lack of actual harm

---

See also "Snowden ally Appelbaum claims his Berlin apartment was invaded," *Deutsche Welle*, 21 December 2013, archive.today/gvdlh

See also Andrew Fowler, Wayne Harley, "Sex, Lies and Julian Assange" (video), *Four Corners*, ABC, 23 July 2012, updated 16 May 2013, archive.today/HCpDj

314. Alexa O'Brien, "WikiLeaks Grand Jury | 7 civilians being target by FBI for #WLGrandJury including #WikiLeaks founders, associates," alexaobrien.com, 21 June 2012, archive.today/cJ0Ho

315. Ed Pilkington, "Bradley Manning's treatment was cruel and inhuman, UN torture chief rules," *Guardian*, 12 March 2012, archive.today/DRcZq

316. Kim Zetter, "Bradley Manning Charged With 22 New Counts, Including Capital Offense," *Wired*, 3 February 2011, archive.today/X6Y4A

resulting from her alleged actions.[317] She offered a limited guilty plea.[318] This plea was refused by the government, which sought to convict Manning on the full charge sheet. The case went to trial in June 2013 in unprecedented secrecy, against which WikiLeaks and the Center for Constitutional Rights litigated. In August 2013 Manning was found guilty on seventeen counts, and sentenced to thirty-five years in prison.[319] At the time of publication, she is appealing her case to the United States Army Court of Criminal Appeals.[320]

CALLS FOR THE ASSASSINATION OF JULIAN ASSANGE AND PUBLICLY DECLARED WIKILEAKS TASK FORCES

The grand jury investigation is not the only avenue of attack on WikiLeaks. In December 2010, in the wake of Cablegate, various US politicians called for the extrajudicial assassination of Julian Assange, including by drone strike. US senators labeled WikiLeaks a "terrorist organization" and named Assange a "high-tech terrorist" and an "enemy combatant" engaged in "cyber warfare."[321]

---

317. Ed Pilkington, "Bradley Manning denied chance to make whistleblower defence," *Guardian*, 17 January 2013, archive.today/Kn8EQ

318. Alexa O'Brien, "Pfc. Manning's Statement for the Providence Inquiry," alexaobrien.com, 28 February 2013, archive.today/Fjjo0

319. Tom McCarthy, "Bradley Manning tells lawyer after sentencing: 'I'm going to be OK'—as it happened," *Guardian*, 21 August 2013, archive.today/kND5Y

320. "Chelsea Manning's 35-year prison sentence upheld by US army general," *Guardian*, 14 April 2014, archive.today/GP08a

321. Nick Collins, "WikiLeaks: guilty parties 'should face death penalty,'" *Telegraph*, 1 December 2010, archive.today/RG81n

A 120-strong US Pentagon team was set up ahead of the release of the Iraq War Logs and Cablegate, dedicated to "taking action" against WikiLeaks.[322] Similar publicly declared task forces in the FBI, the CIA, and the US State Department were also assembled. The US government began to apply pressure to allied countries to detain Julian Assange, and to prevent WikiLeaks from transiting or operating within their territories.[323]

DIRECT CENSORSHIP

In a series of extralegal censorship actions, internet service providers ceased services to wikileaks.org. On December 1, 2010, Amazon removed WikiLeaks from its storage servers, and on December 2 the DNS service pointing to the wikileaks.org domain was disrupted. WikiLeaks was kept online during this period as the result of a "mass-mirroring" effort, whereby thousands of supporters were integrated into a mass-distribution system designed and coordinated by WikiLeaks, offering their servers to host a copy of the website's publications. Thousands of other supporters distributed the IP addresses and alternative domain names for WikiLeaks' site through social networks.[324]

---

322. "DOD News Briefing with Geoff Morrell from the Pentagon" (transcript), US Department of Defense website, 5 August 2010, archive.today/F3CC1
        See also Philip Shenon, "The General Gunning for WikiLeaks," *Daily Beast*, 9 December 2010, archive.today/xx5gK

323. Philip Shenon, "U.S. Urges Allies to Crack Down on WikiLeaks," *Daily Beast*, 8 October 2010, archive.today/Dvkgy

324. Charles Arthur, Josh Halliday, "WikiLeaks fights to stay online after US company withdraws domain name," *Guardian*, 3 December 2010, archive.today/43Jqz

The Obama administration warned federal employees that materials released by WikiLeaks remained classified—even though they were being published by some of the world's leading news organizations including the *New York Times* and the *Guardian*. Employees were told that accessing the material, whether on wikileaks.org or in the *New York Times*, would amount to a security violation. Government agencies such as the Library of Congress, the Commerce and Education Departments, and the US military blocked access to WikiLeaks materials over their networks.[325] The ban was not limited to the public sector. Employees from the US government warned academic institutions that students hoping to pursue a career in public service should stay clear of material released by WikiLeaks in their research and in their online activity.[326]

During the launch of Cablegate, on November 28 and 29, 2010, WikiLeaks came under substantial "distributed denial of service" (DDoS) traffic.[327] The DDoS was not successful in taking WikiLeaks

---

325. Matt Raymond, "Why the Library of Congress is Blocking WikiLeaks," *Library of Congress Blog*, 3 December 2010, archive.today/mVspZ
    See also Ewen MacAskill, "US blocks access to WikiLeaks for federal workers," *Guardian*, 3 December 2010, archive.today/i1LYt
    See also Rowan Scarborough, "Military ordered to stay off WikiLeaks," *Washington Times*, 6 August 2010, archive.today/eZBJk

326. Ewen MacAskill, "Columbia students told job prospects harmed if they access WikiLeaks cables," *Guardian*, 5 December 2010, archive.today/f0vgV

327. Craig Labovitz, "WikiLeaks Cablegate Attack," *Abor Networks IT Security Blog*, 29 November 2010, archive.today/GOYuB
    See also Craig Labovitz, "Round 2: DDoS Versus WikiLeaks," *Abor Networks IT Security Blog*, 30 November 2010, archive.today/CK2Mm

offline, but it did moderately affect the website's availability while the attacks were in session.

SURVEILLANCE AND SUBVERSION CAMPAIGNS AGAINST WIKILEAKS

In 2011 it emerged that Bank of America had, through the law firm Hunton & Williams LLP, commissioned a group of security companies to manage an internal review and external response to WikiLeaks. Leaked internal documents show that one of the security companies, HBGary Federal, proposed "Team Themis"— a private-sector task force including HBGary Federal, Palantir Technologies, and Berico Technologies—which would engage in a campaign of subversion, disinformation, and sabotage against WikiLeaks, its associates, and even supportive third parties, like the journalist Glenn Greenwald.[328]

In early 2014 documents from the National Security Agency obtained by Glenn Greenwald from NSA whistleblower Edward Snowden were published, revealing that the UK's Government Communications Headquarters (GCHQ) had conducted bulk surveillance against every regular visitor to the WikiLeaks website, collecting their IP addresses and search queries in real time. The documents show how GCHQ's Joint Threat Research Intelligence Group (JTRIG) is authorized to perform "Active Covert Internet Operations," "Covert Technical Operations,"

---

328. Nate Anderson, "Spy games: Inside the convoluted plot to bring down WikiLeaks," *Ars Technica*, 14 February 2011, archive.today/wBM2J

and "Effects Operations" against online "adversaries," including infiltrating chat rooms; "false flag" attacks; computer network attacks; DDoS attacks; disruption; jamming phones, computers, and email accounts; and offensive operations intended to "destroy" and "disrupt" adversaries.[329] The same documents showed high-level internal discussions between the office of the NSA's general counsel and other officials about the possibility of designating WikiLeaks a "malicious foreign actor" for the purposes of targeting it.[330]

FINANCIAL CENSORSHIP: THE BANKING BLOCKADE

WikiLeaks is funded by donations from supporters. In December 2010 major banking and financial institutions, including VISA, MasterCard, PayPal, and Bank of America, bowed to unofficial US pressure and began to deny financial services to WikiLeaks. They blocked bank transfers and all donations made with major credit cards.

While these are American institutions, their ubiquity in world finance meant that willing donors in both America and around the world were denied the option of sending money to WikiLeaks to support its publishing activities.

---

329. Mark Schone, Richard Esposito, Matthew Cole, Glenn Greenwald, "War on Anonymous: British Spies Attacked Hackers, Snowden Docs Show," NBC News, 5 February 2014, archive.today/dDR6q

330. Glenn Greenwald, Ryan Gallagher, "Snowden Documents Reveal Covert Surveillance and Pressure Tactics Aimed at WikiLeaks and Its Supporters," *Intercept*, 18 February 2014, archive.today/krpPf

The "banking blockade," as it has become known, is being conducted outside of any judicial or administrative procedure.[331] WikiLeaks has been pursuing major court cases in different jurisdictions across the world in order to break the blockade. The Supreme Court in Iceland found in favor of WikiLeaks in a case against the VISA and MasterCard subsidiary Valitor.[332] A case has been brought to the European Commission, which launched an investigation into the abuse of market dominance by institutions involved in the blockade.[333] The investigation is ongoing at the time of writing. The European Parliament initiated legislation aimed at regulating the financial services market in response to the blockade.[334] A court case in Denmark is in progress.

As of April 2014, the blockade has been significantly eroded as a result of concerted effort by WikiLeaks and its allies. WikiLeaks has managed to arrange ways to donate money via proxy payment gateways, which have not yet been shut down.[335] Some parties to the

---

331. "Banking Blockade," WikiLeaks, 28 June 2011, archive.today/Juoc6

332. "WikiLeaks and DateCell sue Valitor for 9 billion ISK," *News of Iceland*, 5 July 2013, archive.today/pWMBb

333. "European Commission enabling blockade of WikiLeaks by U.S. hard-right Lieberman/King, contrary to European Parliament's wishes," WikiLeaks, 27 November 2012, archive.today/ozC22

334. "European Parliament votes to protect WikiLeaks," WikiLeaks, 20 November 2012, archive.today/AVjUD

335. "Press Release: WikiLeaks opens path through banking siege," WikiLeaks, 18 July 2012, archive.today/Yi41S
    See also "WikiLeaks declares war on banking blockade," WikiLeaks, 16 December 2012, archive.today/9aT0N

blockade have quietly executed a partial or wholesale withdrawal, opening a front for compensation.[336]

SEIZURE OF ELECTRONIC RECORDS

On December 14, 2010, Twitter received an "administrative subpoena" from the US Department of Justice ordering it to give up information that might be relevant to an investigation into WikiLeaks. The subpoena was a so-called 2703(d) order, referring to a section of the Stored Communications Act. Under this law the US government claims the authority to compel the disclosure of private electronic communication records without the need for a judge to issue a search warrant—effectively getting around Fourth Amendment protections against arbitrary search and seizure.

The subpoena sought user names, correspondence records, addresses, telephone numbers, bank account details, and credit card numbers from accounts and people allegedly associated with WikiLeaks, including Julian Assange, security researcher and software developer Jacob Appelbaum, Icelandic parliamentarian Birgitta Jónsdóttir, Dutch businessman and internet pioneer Rop Gonggrijp, Chelsea Manning, and WikiLeaks itself. Under the terms of the subpoena Twitter was gagged from even telling them of the existence of the order. However, Twitter successfully appealed against the gag clause and won the right to inform the targets that their records were being requested.

---

336. "MasterCard breaks ranks in WikiLeaks blockade," WikiLeaks, 3 July 2013, archive.today/boHPO

Once the news of the subpoenas was public, WikiLeaks made a public request that Google and Facebook disclose any similar government subpoenas in relation to the case.[337] Neither company responded.

Having been told about the subpoena by Twitter, on January 26, 2011, Appelbaum, Jónsdóttir, and Gonggrijp—represented by Keker & Van Nest, the American Civil Liberties Union, and the Electronic Frontier Foundation—had their attorneys jointly file a motion to vacate the order. This has become known as the "Twitter subpoena case."[338] A further motion was filed by Appelbaum's attorney requesting to unseal the still-secret court records of the government's attempts to collect his private data from Twitter and any other companies. Both motions were denied by a US magistrate judge on March 11, 2011. The plaintiffs appealed.

On June 23, 2011, in the conversation recorded in this book, Julian Assange personally asked the chairman of Google, Eric Schmidt, to disclose to WikiLeaks any sealed government orders for information pertaining to WikiLeaks or its associates. Schmidt refused, citing gag clauses in government data requests, but said he would pass on a request to Google's legal department. Thereafter, there was no communication from Google concerning government data requests.

On October 9, 2011, the *Wall Street Journal* revealed that the Californian email provider Sonic.net had also received a subpoena demanding the data of Jacob Appelbaum. Sonic had fought the government

---

337. Peter Beaumont, "WikiLeaks demands Google and Facebook unseal US subpoenas," *Guardian*, 8 January 2011, archive.today/HRGYW

338. The case is officially known as "In the Matter of the 2703(d) Order Relating to Twitter Accounts: WikiLeaks, Rop_G, IOERROR; and BirgittaJ."

order and lost, but had obtained permission to disclose that it had been forced to turn over Appelbaum's information. The *Wall Street Journal* also reported that Google had been served a similar subpoena, but did not say whether Google had challenged it in court.[339]

On November 10, 2011, a federal judge decided against Appelbaum, Jónsdóttir, and Gonggrijp, ruling that Twitter must give their information to the Justice Department.[340] On January 20, 2012, the plaintiffs again appealed, seeking to challenge the refusal to unseal orders that might have been sent to companies other than Twitter.[341] On January 23, 2013, the Fourth Circuit Court of Appeals denied the applicants' petition, opining that disclosure of other orders would compromise a criminal investigation being conducted by the government.[342] There was no further appeal.

On June 7, 2013, documents released by NSA whistleblower Edward Snowden revealed the existence of the PRISM program, a classified program giving the NSA access to the private servers of a group of major internet services companies including Microsoft, Skype, Facebook, Apple, and Google.[343]

---

339. Julia Angwin, "Secret Orders Target Email," *Wall Street Journal*, 10 October 2011, archive.today/W0Sla

340. Somini Sengupta, "Twitter Ordered to Yield Data in WikiLeaks Case," *New York Times*, 10 November 2011, archive.today/NTSQb

341. "ACLU & EFF to Appeal Secrecy Ruling in Twitter/WikiLeaks Case" (press release), Electronic Frontier Foundation, 20 January 2012, archive.today/KiVs1

342. "Government demands Twitter records of Birgitta Jonsdottir: 4th Circuit Opinion," Electronic Frontier Foundation, archive.today/3Xfpt

343. Dominic Rushe, James Ball, "PRISM scandal: tech giants flatly deny allowing NSA direct access to servers," *Guardian*, 7 June 2013, archive.today/qAnuF

On June 18, 2013, two Icelandic former WikiLeaks volunteers, Herbert Snorrason and Smári McCarthy, received emails from Google that contained previously sealed court orders and search warrants allowing the seizure of the entire contents of their Gmail accounts by the US government. The orders dated from summer 2011, but Google had waited until their nondisclosure orders had expired, in 2013, before informing both men as to their existence.[344]

Google has not disclosed the existence of similar orders or warrants pertaining to core WikiLeaks staff or associates, but the existence of orders for peripheral figures such as Snorrason and McCarthy indicates that such very likely exist, and remain under seal.

CONCURRENT THREATS

Independent of the US grand jury investigation relating to the publication of documents in 2010, US authorities have launched a concurrent investigation into the 2012 publication of documents from the private intelligence firm Stratfor.

Both the US and the UK governments have initiated criminal proceedings relating to the 2013 publication of classified NSA and GCHQ documents from the whistleblower Edward Snowden. WikiLeaks investigations editor Sarah Harrison, the British citizen who helped Edward Snowden avoid capture by leaving Hong Kong,

---

344. Smári McCarthy, "The Dragnet at the Edge of Forever," smarimccarthy.is, 21 June 2013, archive.today/CLO5x

　　See also Herbert Snorrason, "On Confirmed Assumptions, or, Not Trusting Google is Good Idea," anarchism.is, 21 June 2013, archive.today/bCRkp

has been advised not to return to her home country because of the risk of prosecution there.[345]

ASYLUM

In June 2012, fearing persecution by the United States government, Julian Assange entered the Ecuadorian embassy in London and formally requested asylum.[346]

After two months of consideration, during which the UK government threatened to forcefully enter the embassy, thereby violating the Vienna Convention, the Ecuadorian government formally found that the US pursuit of Julian Assange and WikiLeaks constituted persecution under the terms of international law.[347] Julian Assange was granted asylum.[348]

At the date of publication, Julian Assange has remained at Ecuador's London embassy for two years, deprived by the UK government of his right to safe passage to his host country.

345. Sarah Harrison, "Britain is treating journalists as terrorists—believe me, I know," *Guardian*, 14 March 2014, archive.today/gACHR

346. For background, see "Extraditing Assange," justice4assange.com, archive.today/y3NPZ#WHAT

347. "Britain's threat to Ecuador 'without precedent,' says international law expert," *Australian*, 16 August 2012, archive.today/43OD2

348. "Ecuador grants asylum to Julian Assange" (press conference), *WikiLeaks Press*, 16 August 2012, archive.today/oH8Au

ACKNOWLEDGMENTS

My dearest thanks go to: the team at WikiLeaks, Sarah, Joseph, Kristinn, and the many others—equally irreplaceable—who nevertheless cannot be named; our friends in the public, who have kept us going; our allies, who know who they are; our lawyers, who are now numerous but all of whom I appreciate greatly; Eric, Jared, Lisa, and Scott, for encouraging me to put pen to paper; Ecuador and its people, who have been good to me, and without whose protection I could not have written this work; E.I. and B.H., who have put many sleepless nights into making it happen; everyone at OR Books, especially Colin, John, and Alex, for their patience and support; and to those fighting for their liberty—Chelsea Manning, Jeremy Hammond, Barrett Brown, Rudolf Elmer, Gottfrid Svartholm Warg, Peter Sunde Kolmisoppi, John Kiriakou, Edward Snowden, the PayPal 14, and those anonymous others of courage and conscience who continue to be an inspiration.

NOTE ON REFERENCES

To insure against "link rot," most of the web pages cited in this book have been referenced using the archiving service **archive.today**

Visit the **archive.today** link in the footnote to find the reference to the original web page.

In the event that **archive.today** itself becomes unavailable, a copy of each of these links is available at **when.google.met.wikileaks.org**

To get to the copy, just replace **archive.today** in the link with **when.google.met.wikileaks.org**

For instance, for the link **archive.today/r2rur**, just type **when.google.met.wikileaks.org/r2rur**

An archive of all the references can be found using this magnet link: **magnet:?xt=urn:btih:744ac8007e1e72e99fc27c561916b3b48daef743**

JULIAN ASSANGE is the publisher of WikiLeaks. He has received numerous awards as a journalist and has authored hundreds of investigations relating to corruption, war, and the surveillance industry. Prior to founding WikiLeaks, Assange specialized in developing encryption software. Julian Assange received political asylum in 2012 as a result of the ongoing US Department of Justice probe into WikiLeaks. He is currently living in the Ecuadorian embassy in London under the protection of the government of Ecuador. He is the author of *Cypherpunks: Freedom and the Future of the Internet* (OR Books, 2012) and other books.

CPSIA information can be obtained
at www.ICGtesting.com
Printed in the USA
JSHW031523180721
16914JS00002B/3

9 781944 869113